Awakening to
Your Story

Awakening to Your Story

Alicia Hartzell

KAYAK PRESS
Austin · Texas

First Published in the United States in 2013 by
Kayak Press, Austin, Texas.

ISBN: 978-0-9912421-7-7

LCCN: 2013921905

Kayak Press is a wholly owned subsidiary of Awakening to Your Story.

For information email alicia@awakeningtoyourstory.com,
or visit us at www.awakeningtoyourstory.com

This book is designed to provide information and motivation to its readers. It is sold with
the understanding that the publisher is not engaged to render any type of psychological,
legal, or any other kind of professional advice. The content of this book is the sole
expression and opinion of its author. No warranties or guarantees are expressed or
implied. Neither the publisher nor the individual author shall be liable for any physical,
psychological, emotional, financial, or commercial damages, including, but not limited to,
special, incidental, consequential, or other damages. Our views and rights are the same:
You are responsible for your own choices, actions, and results.

The events and characters in this book are composites of several individual events or
persons. The names of characters and locations used as examples in this book have been
changed, as have certain physical characteristics and other descriptive details.
Any resemblance to actual persons or events is purely coincidental.

Packaged for Kayak Press by Mulberry Tree Press, Inc.
Manufactured in the United States of America.
FIRST EDITION

Dedicated to you, the brilliant person reading this book.
It was written for you, because your story
is more valuable than you realize.

My appreciation goes out to my people,
you know who you are.

Thank you for being with me on this river of life and
for being such a beautiful part of my story.

Reaction — a boat which is going against the current but which does not prevent the river from flowing on.

—Victor Hugo

Contents

Awakening to
Your Story

PART ONE

Changing Your Perspective

VERY ONE OF US HAS A UNIQUE AND POWERFUL STORY that is his or hers alone. Learning to be alert to and embrace that story can fill our lives with joy and richness that we all deserve. *Awakening to Your Story* was created to help you awaken to all that your story offers. You will walk through constructive approaches that, when practiced, can bring about endless positive change within your life. From time to time, we all experience setbacks from emotional pain, struggle, heartbreak, failure, confusion, stagnation, depression, anxiety, frustration, or other nagging emotional issues. Some of these setbacks can be devastatingly deep. *Awakening to Your Story* will give you the valuable tools needed to put these experiences to work for you, to guide you into a place of harmony.

What makes *Awakening to Your Story* different is that it not only gives you information, it also helps you get started, and gives you actions you can take that empower you to create movement within your life. Reading these pages, you will obtain the tools to enact positive changes in your life, and the strength, motivation, and knowledge to use those tools. You can start today.

It all begins by changing your perspective. Think about challenging experiences that you have faced. I am sure that you can come up with a few. As you reflect on the circumstances surrounding these challenges, you may focus on how they affected you outwardly. You may even feel yourself reacting emotionally at just the thought of the event. This reaction is telling you that it is time to make a shift.

The shift in perspective goes from one that looks outward at all the information happening to you, to one that looks inward at all the information that is there to help you. As your perspective starts to shift inward, your capacity to hold positive and brilliant experiences will begin to expand. Because your shifting perspective is directly linked to your capacity to make positive change in your life; the more you shift, the greater the positive change.

In Part One of *Awakening to Your Story* you will look at what it means to bring consciousness into the process of life and truly awaken to your story. You will also look at the importance of living only *your* life and begin to understand and create a new relationship with the information in your story.

CHAPTER 1

Awakening to Your Story

E VERY PERSON WHO HAS LIVED on this planet we call Earth has a unique story. No one has lived a life exactly like any other. Consider how incredible that is. From the beginning of time, people have lived and have taken in all of the information that has surrounded them. With that information, each person created a story that differs completely from that of anyone else. Each person has his or her own individual story, and the point at which he or she awakens to that story is just as unique.

In this chapter, you will explore the meaning of awakening to your story. As you begin to examine awakening, you return to a place where your mind and heart are working together. Awakening to your story is about becoming conscious. By looking at how you have processed your information throughout your life, you can begin to see contrast and find understanding within yourself. After you become aware of how you have processed and are currently processing information, you can start to see information for what it represents in your life. Then, rather than simply living through or surviving your life by reacting to the information in your story, you can instead interact with and completely engage with the information, and use it to move forward. As these ideas unfold and settle in, the chapters ahead will help illustrate what awakening can look like.

When you were born and embarked on becoming part of this world, you were extremely present. Your needs or wants at any particular moment held your complete attention. After those current needs were met, you had the freedom to move on to your next need or want. There was no baggage or filter in this place; you just *were*. When you were in this open place of just being, you were completely connected and brilliantly conscious. Research shows that children are more openly connected to the higher consciousness than adults. There is an element of this found in many belief systems.

Imagine that, before you were born, you had the opportunity to choose a broad spectrum of experiences that you hoped to encounter and learn from in the life you would be creating. When connected to the higher consciousness, you know what this particular life and story will teach you. Once you are born and begin to interact with your surroundings, you begin to gather the information that you will need to learn and grow. By stepping into this information, you can then live completely into your story. Gathering information is an immediate process. For many, your first experience was latching on to your mother to learn how to eat. From there, you learned that your mother provided food for you, and thus began the early gathering of information for your story.

In this first phase, your world is small. You have parents or others who take care of you. Your world barely extends beyond your home environment. You eat, digest your food, cry to let people know what you need, and you sleep. In most cases, someone is there to provide for you, to give you food and comfort you when you cry. You start to grow, and as you do, take in the world around you little bits a time. You learn your name; you learn language, to speak and understand.

You continue to grow and progress through developmental stages in which you actively learn how to engage more directly with the information around you. You go through a "my" phase around the ages of two to four. It's "*my* toy" and "*my* book." You even say that people *belong* to you. As a child, you might say, "That's *my* mommy" or "*my* brother." You use these statements and make these differentiations in order to define who you are. At that young age, you are already beginning to process the information around you and realize that it is your own. If you take a moment to watch a child, you will notice their curiosity. They observe and take in everything around them, gathering as much information as they can and just as naturally letting it go.

When you are young, there are so many new things to uncover. The world happens around you, and you are overjoyed to dig in and see how it all works. As you age, you lose that childlike sense of curiosity and adventure, therefore your ability to experience life feels dulled. As you get older, the amount of information you are exposed to increases and you often take in this information more quickly than you can process it. You engage, triumph, fail, learn, and discover, as you find your place in it all.

By the time you begin to tiptoe into adulthood, the amount of information that comes into your life has changed, and you feel as if things are happening *to* you instead of *for* you. This change might happen long before adulthood. You eventually find yourself surrounded by piles of information from your past. Because of these piles, your ability to process and engage the new information with curiosity gets stunted. You become limited and defined by this old information. As more new information comes in, it collides with the old piles of information. You are no longer able to consciously engage the current information because you get lost in the old information that has accumulated around you. You lose the sense that life is an adventure of discovery because you are overwhelmed by these old piles of information. Because of this, rather than interacting with the new information that comes into your everyday life, you find yourself reacting to it as is it jams up against these old piles. The piles get larger and you begin to feel uncomfortable in the life you are living. You wonder why things are happening to you, and how you got to this place where your life feels so difficult. There is no longer space for conscious curiosity and adventure.

It's here that you willingly give your information away. As the piles continue to grow out of the realm of conscious interaction, you begin to hand the new information over to others. This is where you find yourself believing that things happen *to* you instead of *for* you. You begin to replay scenarios over and over in your head, waiting for an outcome that reflects all the crap that has accumulated in the piles of information around you. You interact and engage with the world through the old piles of information. New information comes in, but to address it at all, it must go through the older piles before it gets to your core. As you engage with the outside world, you find yourself frustrated and stuck. This is because, to put something out into the world, it too must travel through the piles of old information.

As a pendulum swings from one side to the other, it wants to return. You might find yourself simply overwhelmed and longing for some sense of freedom, or you might be tired, angry, or resentful. The welling up of these experiences creates enough contrast to what you once knew that you begin to let the pendulum swing back. This is where you begin to awaken to your story. This is where the real fun and adventure starts.

For every unique story, there is an equally unique awakening. Awakening to your story is the place where you turn the volume down on the old information that lays in piles around you, and you turn the volume up on where and who you are today. Awakening to your story is becoming conscious and living into the adventure that awaits you with every step you take. The life you chose, and have lived into every day since, starts to feel as if it is perfectly falling into place. As you awaken to your story and your consciousness, you begin to feel that you are part of something bigger. You begin to see how every interaction in life settles into its perfect place.

As you shift and wake up to the brilliance of your story, you can slowly navigate through the piles of old information. You were there once before. Before the information started flooding in and the piles started to gather, you were completely connected. As you awaken to your story, you return to the place of being connected to the higher consciousness. The reality is that you were never actually disconnected, but with the piles of information in the way, you lost your awareness of that connection.

Awakening to your story can come on quickly. It might be initiated by a dramatic or tragic incident. It might simply begin by building up enough contrast in your story to catapult you into an awakened place. It may happen slowly over years. You may tiptoe in and out of a conscious place in your story before you fully engage in all that it has to offer you. Whatever the first steps are that lead you into a place of waking up to your story, know that it's yours. No one else's story is written in the same way that yours is, and no one's awakening is lived out the same way yours is. Live into that unique place that is carved out just for you. This is *your* story and *your* awakening. How your story develops and how you live into it is completely up to you. You are the author of your life, and you get to live it in the way that you want to. You are able to embrace or let go of any information in your story. As you navigate through information, past and present, the relationship you have with your own heart grows stronger. As this strengthens, you find yourself living more from a place of harmony, where you are connected to the higher consciousness. No matter what finds its way into your story, you are able to use it as information that will lead you deeper into your story and closer to your happiness and harmony. You no longer have to give away your information, or project old information and patterns onto others.

Let's look at some examples of what awakening can look like. I also want to illustrate how information can pile up and manifest in a story. For some of you reading this, the understanding is clear. It resonates with you, and you may feel as if, somehow, you were reading something specifically written for you. For others, the abstract idea is not enough for you to see it clearly. It may also be that the piles of information around you have not quite created enough contrast for you to resonate with the information yet. Try to stay engaged with curiosity.

This book is designed to help you awaken to your story, as well as navigate through the information, both old and new. The examples that follow demonstrate some of the tools that are used in the chapters ahead. Although they may start to sound exciting to you, you may not have enough information from the examples here to get you where you want to go. The principle and tools are clearly defined in the chapters ahead so that you can pick them up and use them to help you awaken and live into your story.

I would like to introduce you to Avery and William. Each has begun to awaken to their stories. I chose a man and a woman to illustrate that awakening to your story and using this process is not gender-specific. Avery is a smart, creative woman who has a caring husband and beautiful children. William is a brilliant businessman who travels the world, creating business ventures. Both found themselves in unsettling situations, in what I like to call "hiccups" in their lives.

Avery's Story

LET'S START WITH AVERY. On the outside, Avery's life was picturesque. She had a husband who loved and supported her in all that she did. He was able to make enough money so that she could raise their children in their beautiful home that they had created together. She had two bright and gifted girls who were happy and healthy. They were able to take vacations as a family. They carved out time to make their family a priority. They had sit-down dinners and bike rides to the park. Every Sunday, they walked to the neighborhood coffee shop and talked about the upcoming week.

On many levels, there was happiness—or what she felt was happiness—but she caught herself saying things like "I should feel lucky." She also noticed that she had started having a short fuse with the girls. They would bicker, or make a mess of something, and she would feel so angry that it felt out of character for her. She would feel her blood pressure rise, along with her voice, as she tried to get the girls to behave. She had gone to her husband to talk about it and he tried to fix things for her, but this only left her feeling even angrier. She found herself constantly frustrated, and she knew that if she didn't do something it would continue to worsen. She dreaded the outings with her family that should have been fun. She would sit at Sunday morning coffee wishing she could be at home by herself. The frustration and anger were beginning to feel like part of normalcy, and she didn't like it. She did not want to resent her family, but it was getting harder and harder not to.

Avery was interacting with her children and husband through old piles of information that she had gathered from previous moments in her life. When she yelled at and reprimanded her girls, she was interacting with them through old information. She had no idea why she would get so triggered by what the girls were doing. Was it really that bad for them to have all their doll clothes out when they were playing? Did they really need to take only one thing out at a time? Was it so important for them to play quietly? Why couldn't they laugh and act things out in a full, fun, loud manner?

Avery began to awaken to her story when she felt the contrast in her life. She felt the growing chasm between happiness and frustration. She remembered a time when there was more joy than frustration. She recognized the difference between interacting with her family from that place of joy versus the growing place of anger. As she began to open up to her story and live into the information around her, she was able to see the piles of old information around her. She could not define or name them all, but she could see them and feel them there. Once she noticed them, she could see the present information having to fight its way through the old information. Avery's awakening started slowly and came about because of contrast in the old and new information. Now, as she looked at the new information without the filter of the old information, the picture was very different. For her, the new information was that her children were happy and curious.

When they had all their doll clothes laid out on the floor, it meant that they liked seeing the big picture. They enjoyed having options, and they wanted to be surrounded by those options. What a great trait for a person to have! When they were dancing and acting out their plays, they were so free and happy. They were fully engaged and scared of nothing. It was as if they could not make a mistake as they linked one scene to another. As she looked at her children without the old information as a filter, she could see what amazing people they were becoming. That was the place from which she wanted to parent. She didn't want to get lost in the frustration and stifle her children's joy.

For Avery to use the contrast, and move toward parenting and living in the way that she wanted, she needed to use some of the old information in the piles. It was not enough to recognize the contrast. She had to awaken further to her story. She tiptoed into it by navigating though the old information and was able to identify the first time in her life that she felt this kind of frustration. She was able to find a time in her childhood when all she wanted to do was play in the giant mud puddles in her front yard. She went outside, took off her shoes, and before she could even get her feet dirty, her mother was scolding her. As she thought back, she could see that same sort of frustrated energy. In the memory, she felt it herself, but she also felt it radiating from her mother.

She knew that her mother loved her even though their relationship had always been a little strained. She thought back on those years in general and found that her mother was constantly more concerned with seeing if Avery was doing something wrong than that she was with showing Avery any affection. Her curiosity and sense of freedom were always nipped in the bud.

"Why aren't you . . . ?"

"You should have . . ."

"Don't you ever think before you . . . ?"

These were all tag lines that came flooding to her in her mother's voice. She was able to navigate back to that time, and realized that her mother had given this old pile of information to her.

Avery was engaging with her children through that old information. It was as if there was a small wound that had not healed. The conscious woman of today went back to that moment of repression and allowed her child self to jump in the mud puddles. She stood by and watched how much fun she was having and could feel the freedom washing over her. She walked up to the girl and told her how beautiful she was covered in dirt, and that she was so proud of her for having such a wild sense of adventure. She was able to give herself the love and acceptance that her mother couldn't. Once she was able to do that, she could let go of the old information that she had gathered from her mother, and shift the space in her heart where the wound had been created. From there, she was free to live into her current information. She was so much happier because she was in harmony with her heart. The anger and frustration melted away, and she was able to interact with her children in a way that brought her joy and made her more balanced. Because she was able to reduce the piles of old information in her life, her parenting became less reactive and more engaged.

In this illustration, you can see that living with piles of old information can be very daunting. It makes sense that a large portion of our society struggles with depression and anger management issues. Whether you have created strong contrast and you are facing some major challenges in your life, or the contrast is gentle but you just don't feel your life is in the place where you want it to be, there is freedom waiting for you in the details of your story. All you have to do is engage with the information right at your fingertips. It is there for you because it is your story. All you have to do is awaken to it.

William's Story

WILLIAM'S STORY IS GOING TO CREATE SOME BALANCE for us. In many ways, our society believes that a man should be the picture of strength. In that picture of strength, there is little room for emotional fallibility. Men and women have evolved with essential dissimilarities. Because of differing hormonal structures, the undercurrent of how men and women process information is also quite distinct. While the undercurrent, or force, with which the information is processed may vary, the fact still remains that the information is there for both genders to utilize as part of their stories. The way in which William awakened to his story will help you see that the information and the structure for engaging it is the same for both genders.

Much like Avery, William's life seemed perfect. He was a handsome businessman who spent most of his time traveling the world. He worked hard, and believed in playing equally hard. He created a successful global business, and had been able to start venturing into the world of philanthropy more and more. His life was filled with people who loved him and whom he loved. From the outside, a person could not ask for much more. The start to William's awakening was a little more subtle than Avery's. He had not created great contrast between joy and anger, happiness and frustration. The contrast in William's awakening was a bit more delicate.

William had created a full life for himself. There was never a dull moment and most of the information that he called in seemed to work in his favor. William was in his forties at the time. He had created a couple of long-term relationships with wonderful women, but he never found himself settled into a relationship where the thought of marriage made sense to him. He created loving relationships, but what he was creating with his business always seemed to take top priority in his life.

He was coming home from one of his trips overseas when he began to feel the slightest nudge of contrast. He walked into his house and went about his normal unpacking routine. He finished, and opened all the doors along the back of the house to get the stale air moving and let the fresh air in. He poured himself a glass of wine and sat on the deck. As he watched the sunset, he felt a twinge of emptiness. There seemed to be a longing of some sort. It was subtle, but it lingered until he went to sleep that night. When he woke up, he noticed it was still there. The best he could tell was that he needed to connect. He was a smart man, so he decided to do just that. He called up a good friend and scheduled a golf game and lunch. He was able to connect enough to satisfy part of the longing. They laughed and talked business. They both played an excellent round of golf. He left the club feeling content. By they time he made it home, that twinge was right back in the same place. It felt as if something were missing, but he could not put his finger on what it was. He was a man who often got to the roots of problems and came up with effective solutions. Why wasn't he getting to the root of this little thing? This went on for a couple of weeks. He tried plugging different things in to fill the empty space, but nothing seemed to work for very long. It took him a while to get out of his head and into his heart. He needed to do that before he could understand that there was enough contrast to create a shift, and an awakening, within his story. He had gotten to a place where he could not keep himself busy enough to keep the feeling of connection going. It was time for William to broaden his perspective and see the old information that he was living through for what it was.

William's current information was that he was extremely connected in his life. He was surrounded by love, joy, and laughter. However, William was interacting with that information through the piles of old information around him. Intellectually, this idea of old piles of information made sense to him. He wanted to get to the root of the situation, and this process seemed to fall into place at just the right time for him. It could not hurt to try it. From here, he began to awaken to his story. He navigated back to the old information through which he had been interacting.

When he first saw it, he thought that it was too obvious. He wondered if what was coming up for him could really be the information that he needed to acknowledge. He was stunned at how obvious it all seemed. When he looked back, he found himself at nine years old, sitting in a hospital waiting room. He could tell that something was wrong, but no one was telling him anything. That morning, his mom, dad, and brother had gone to see him play in a baseball game. The boys decided to go out for ice cream, and his mother was going to take the opportunity to go to the store on her own. As he sat and remembered, he noticed that it had not been that long from the time they left their mother at the ball field to the moment in which he found himself in the waiting room, yet it seemed like forever. As he looked back into the memory, he could see his sweet little face turned down to his feet with his arm over his little brother's shoulder. He could feel the separation happening in his chest as he sat there worried, not knowing what was happening. He noticed that it was the same place in his chest where he had been feeling that twinge for the last couple of weeks. He returned to the memory. His aunt came into the waiting room and took both of them home. She would not say what was going on. She just put them in the back of the car and took them home. Later that night, his dad came home and sat both boys on the couch. He told them that their mother had been in an accident on the way home from the store, and that she had died. He would never see her again. He thought about it for a moment. Looking back on the memory, he felt just as stunned now as he did back then. He knew that this was not new information. He sat in the stunned and separated feeling for a few moments. He had assumed that knowing that it had happened was enough. It was something that had happened, and nothing he could do today could change the fact that she was gone, and that she had missed the rest of his life. William could not change that fact of his story. He could, however, interact with both the old information and the new information.

William had been interacting through an old pile of information that taught him that people you love will leave you without saying good-bye. Their leaving creates a hole so big that you can't imagine trying to fill it because it just can't be filled. Years later, his father married a wonderful woman and she stepped into his life with love and tenderness. She became a wonderful mother figure for him, but there was a wound that didn't seem to heal, and that wound accumulated information that William had been using to protect himself from being hurt again. Because of the level of tenderness that his stepmother was able to give him, the wound was masked, just as he had been masking the feeling of separation for years.

Once he was able to see the old pile of information for what it was, he was able to go back to the place where the little boy was in the waiting room and talk with him about loss and love. The conscious William of today walked that very young version of himself back to the moment the wound was created. The two of them went back to see his mother. He was able to see her body on the hospital bed. He could put the pieces of time together from that day. He could feel this allowing him to be more connected to the time he felt he had lost. He then took the boy back further into the memory of that day, and allowed him to hug his mother again, to touch her. He was able to say good-bye, feel her arms around him, and smell her lavender perfume. He could hear her whispering into his ear that she would always and forever love him. He kissed her cheek and whispered back that he loved her always and forever. He asked her why she had to go. She held his hands and said that it was her time and that she had learned the things that she came to learn. He begged her not to go. She asked him if he wanted to know a secret. He nodded his head, yes. She said "You and your brother have been the best part of my life. The love that we have created has been the best part of who I am. I can leave here knowing that the best part of me is still here in you. We will always be part of each other.

Find and create more love the way you have learned, so that what we have created can keep moving forward. Don't be fooled that I have ever left you." The William of today was able to go back and help the William who had gathered the old information to now navigate through it. He was able to show the boy that his mother would forever be a part of him.

By consciously being there for that younger and wounded part of himself, William was able to experience just how connected to love he was. Not only was he connected to the love that he and his mother created, but he was also truly connected to his own heart. By going back, he learned that his mother had actually taught him just how strong love was. His mother had taught him how to love, and now he was going to love himself, and live into his story in that same way.

William realized that he had not allowed himself to fully engage in a relationship with a woman because he had been living through that old pile of information. There was a part of him that believed that if he connected that deeply to another person, in the end he would be left alone. It could only leave him feeling hurt, with a gaping hole where love once was. Once he was able to give the old information the room it needed, the pile disappeared. The old information no longer fit. He had shifted it, creating room for the new information to flow in more freely. The details of the story were still there, but his new information no longer had to push its way through it.

Now that he had awakened to the truth within his story, he could see a path that would allow him to fully connect to unconditional love again. He had it within him, and he was creating it for himself. He could create it just as his mother had shown him. He had created it with her, and now that the wound was cleared, he could create it again with other people. He no longer felt the twinge of emptiness because he had filled it with love. There was no longer a need to hide from unconditional love or put obstacles in the way of creating it. He could see the contrast in how he had engaged in love before and the freedom he was feeling in the understanding of love now. With this new freedom, he could move forward and create the unconditional love that he had quietly been longing for. He had awakened to his story, and this was just the beginning. He had begun to harmonize his heart, and could move forward with the ability to fully engage with his

information. Old or new, the information was his, and he could unconditionally love, and be there to engage in every amazing detail of his story.

Avery and William let us see how awakening to your story can play out.
With every story, there are parts of the awakening process that are unique
to only that story. But in every awakening process, your capacity to love
grows. Your ability to embrace and enjoy your life expands. Harmony is
yours if you only wake up to all that is within your glorious story.

Just by reading these words, you are broadening your ability to engage
differently with the information around you. As you begin to rub the
sleep from your eyes and wake up to something new, remember to be
tender with yourself. When you see the piles of old information around
you, take your time with them. The information will come up gently, as
you need it. Your heart will call in new information that will illuminate
the old information that is longing to be shifted. There is no need to jump
in and stir everything up all at once. Just take it as it comes, and know
that it is all there for you.

CHAPTER 2

Living Only "Your" Life

A S YOU AWAKEN TO YOUR STORY, it is important to work toward living your own life. It sounds like a simple task, but it may be more difficult than you think. In order to differentiate between whose information is whose, you must first become conscious of the distractions you face. As you go through this chapter, you will begin to see how you end up living into other people's stories while also living your life through your old information. We will shine a light on how projections and expectations limit you from fully engaging with your information. Once you have a broader understanding of how the distractions work, we will move on to an example that includes recognizing and claiming information. It will help to illustrate what living your own life can look like, while exemplifying how invigorating and empowering this new kind of living can be.

Without even recognizing it, most people attempt to live into other people's stories and lives. This can manifest itself in the many different ways as you talk to yourself and hear others:

"Do it this way, so that it is easier for you and for me."

"Be this person."

"Act this way, so that I can be happy."

By thinking like this, you are actually working your way into someone else's story. You ask people to do all sorts of things for you: feel this emotion, hold this place in my life, be this particular image that I have in my mind, and other self-centered requests. You may not realize it, but by placing unspoken demands on others, you are attempting to live into their story. You are trying to control or direct details of their lives for them, which provides an illusion that you are in control of your own life. It also distracts you from navigating through, and living into, your own story completely.

So how did you get to a place where you were separated from living only your own story?

Getting Distracted By Other People's Information

TAKE A MOMENT TO DIG INTO THIS IDEA to see if you can find a new perspective. When engaging in the details of other people's lives, you can't possibly know all of their information. You have not even gone through the piles of information in your own story. You can no more control someone else's life than you could paddle the Titanic up a stream in only five feet of water. The attempt will only cause you to be tired and frustrated. Living in someone else's story leaves you even more separated from your own information, heart, and story.

Now, take a step back and look at your individual story as it relates information coming in. As your new information comes in and bumps up against or has to filter through the old piles of information, it is very easy to be distracted. You may react to new information as a response to the old info. This reaction can cause you to project things from your past onto something that you are experiencing in the present moment with another person. When this happens, the details may truly feel as if they are pertinent to the other person's story, when really they belong to your story. By shifting the focus onto someone else's story, you find yourself inevitably giving information away that is designed to help you. Because you can never truly live other people's lives for them, your attempts to live into their lives leaves you feeling conflicted, confused, and once again, frustrated.

Attempting to Control the Information

AS YOU CAN IMAGINE, when there are many old piles of information cluttering up your consciousness, there might be a part of you that will try to regain some control. This leads you to attempt to direct everything that comes in, so that you can keep all the piles of information organized. However, in the end, orchestrating the information only makes it more difficult for you to live your life. As you awaken to your story and begin to sift through the old piles of information, you'll feel less of a desire to control the information coming in. Rather than reacting to and struggling to rewrite the details and interactions in your life, you can attend to sifting through each pile of old info that presents itself to you, as it comes up. This conscious and refocused attention to the old information can eradicate, or at least reduce, the limiting and distracting desire to control the details of the new information coming into your life.

Limiting Ourselves Through Projections and Expectations

NOT ONLY IS IT IMPORTANT TO RECOGNIZE your own information and separate it from others', it is equally important to let go of expectations; both the ones that are projected onto you, and the ones that you project onto others. Letting go of expectations and projections opens up the doorway for you to successfully find and claim as your own the information that comes into your life. Whether you are projecting your reality onto others or find yourself on the receiving end, it is important to bring your conscious awareness to the information so you can understand the influence that expectation and projection have on keeping you from living into your story.

Getting caught up in expectations and being distracted by other people's information instead of focusing on your own is not unusual. Meet Tabitha and Max. Their stories illustrate how easy it is to get lost in other people's information, as well as how simple it can be to shift your perspective inward and use what is happening in your life to shift your old info out. Tabitha's example shows you that as you claim your information, you get to interact with it rather than react to it. She also helps you see where projections can sneak into your perception of your story. Max's example helps you see what it is like to identify information that, at first, may not feel like it is your own. Both illustrations may help you lean toward shifting your perspective inward so you can begin to live *your* life, and *only your* life, leading you toward a more harmonious place from which to narrate and live into your story.

Tabitha's Story

TABITHA GREW UP WITH TWO SISTERS who were born within a five-year time period. They were as close emotionally as they were in age. To the outside world the family appeared a tight-knit crew. The girls' reality was very different. Behind closed doors, the girls dealt with abuse and dysfunction. They all had grown up under the same roof, but each survived her childhood trauma in a very different way. Each woman had her own information that she gathered along the way. Some of the information was similar, and some was dramatically different. As they became adults, the piles of information that they had collected began to stack up, and each of them lived with the information differently. Even though they had experienced the same events at the same time, the information each had collected was different, and how they dealt with that information was also different. Their lives therefore diverged, and their perceptions of the shared events of their lives varied as well.

As you can imagine, because they had lived together for over twenty years, Tabitha and her sisters had lots of old information that bumped up against each other's and caused some friction. Lots of things fed into their patterns of interaction; birth order, gender, parental favorites, to name a few. As Tabitha looked farther into the old piles of information that had gathered from their youth, it was hard for her to tell whose information belonged to whom. Tabitha loved her sisters deeply and wanted to protect them even when she was barely surviving her own adolescence.

As they all moved into adulthood, Tabitha's longing to help them only grew. If something was not working in their lives, she would worry desperately about it. She would try to come up with ways to help them feel better. She would get caught up in their stories without even realizing that she was doing it. Tabitha thought she was being the helpful big sister. She had no idea that a person could over-care or over-love someone by trying to fix the problems or hiccups in their stories. By constantly offering solutions or advice meant to make their lives simpler or safer, Tabitha was acting as if she knew their lives better than they did. That made them react to her love with anger and resentment. She loved her sisters so much, but she just didn't know how to interact with them without getting their information tangled up in her own. Tabitha's old piles of information at this point had gotten pretty overwhelming, and she was not conscious that she was trying to take on their information as well. Her intentions were good, but her actions were leading her farther away from her own happiness and causing friction in her relationships.

Once Tabitha was able to stop being distracted by her sisters' information, she was able to navigate through her own. From that place, she was able to see that her job was not to help them change or alter the details of their lives. Nor was it her job to protect them from the world around them. Her only job as their sister was to love them. Plain and simple, *just love them.* Once she was untangled from the distraction of their information and was able to begin to move through her own, she found that she could love them with a freedom that she had never really felt in her childhood. She could now love them unconditionally without all the reactions and distractions of the old information. She was free to love her sisters completely for who they were instead of trying to control the details of their lives to make them who she wanted them to be.

Tabitha awoke to the understanding that the information that came into her sisters' lives belonged to them and was meant for their stories, not hers. In turn, she was able to navigate through the piles of old information in her own life, which allowed her to finally interact with her sisters from a more liberated place. When Tabitha recognized how important her information was to her life's story, she could see how important their information was to their own stories. From there, no matter what crazy detail popped up, Tabitha could stand by them in support while they navigated their way through it. Now that the distraction and confusion of information had been sorted out in her mind and heart, she was able to let go of expectations that she had unfairly projected onto them or their relationships. As she let go of those projections, her sisters got to be the beautiful people that they were, and she got to love them unconditionally as those people. Tabitha's evolution was focused inward, working on and harmonizing her own heart, which allowed her to become a better sister.

Tabitha had to navigate through the subtle expectations that she had unconsciously placed on her sisters. They were so subtle that her sisters might not have even consciously understood them. One expectation manifested as a projection of a need to find truth. They had each survived so much through their childhoods, and she expected them to dig into the information and find their truth and direction in the same way that she did. "Remain single, sort through your information, and for heaven's sake don't repeat the mistakes that our parents made," she admonished silently and secretly. She caught herself thinking, "Stop and find your truth the way that I am and you can be happy like me." Interestingly, she was not really all that happy at the time. She was merely projecting her own version of what happiness looked like on them. If they could only find out how all their pieces fit, then they would be closer to happiness (her version) and they would not have to relive or reenact the trauma they had endured as children. She was projecting expectations all over them without even knowing it. In essence, Tabitha was fighting against her own piles of information as well as fighting against the stories of her sisters. By projecting her information into their stories, she ended up literally fighting against them. Tabitha was paddling her boat against the current, and she was simultaneously trying to jump into their boats and paddle for them. You can only live your own story; you cannot live someone else's for them.

Tabitha's sisters' stories are perfect for them, just as your story is perfect for you. Every last thing that you call in is a brilliant representation of information hidden in your heart. Though Tabitha's sisters lived under the same roof with her, they did not have the same experiences as Tabitha. They did not take away information that was identical, nor did they survive the information in the same way. Everything that had come up in their lives had come up to help them lift up the old information that they lived through. With the shift in perspective, Tabitha could differentiate between information. Her job as a sister didn't include navigating through their lives for them because only they could know the nooks and crannies of their own stories. Tabitha could see that her only job as a sister was and is to love them.

Another part of eliminating expectations is letting go of those projected onto you by others, or even by yourself. Sometimes those are more challenging to see because they can be so deeply rooted in your old information. For Tabitha, the expectations that she placed on herself were directly linked to how she survived the old information. When her parents were incapable of parenting or were out of the picture, it was up to her to love her sisters and make sure they were all safe and had what they needed. Even as things began to shift in the household, in many ways she still felt as if she had some sort of responsibility for caring for them. As they got older, they became even more successful than she was at accomplishing the things that they wanted. She was so proud of them and what they were able to make happen for themselves. They were becoming such responsible, smart, capable people. But, the expectation to take care of them was still there in the piles of old information that Tabitha had gathered and was carrying.

As she shifted out of the expectations that she had projected onto them, she also needed to shift out of the expectations that she had placed on herself. For her to fully live into her own story, she had to let got of the old piles of information that had her tied to her sisters' stories. Tabitha had to recognize that, while they had survived their childhood together, she was not responsible for anyone's happiness but her own. She was not responsible for anyone's information but her own. She went back to the seven-year-old version of herself and sat with her, and let her know that she could love them and let go of anything that felt painful or burdensome between them. It was okay to let go of it all. She cut the old cords and navigated her way through the old information, only holding on to love. She was able to create unconditional love that no longer had to be filtered through old information and old expectations. Tabitha was no longer tied to her sisters because of a sense of duty or responsibility, but she was tied to them because of a love and appreciation that she had for who they were. Clearing through the old information allowed her to live into her life and let go of the need to live into anyone else's. As she began living into her own story and started claiming her information, she was able to harmonize her heart and feel the freedom and endless possibility that her story offered her.

Moving through the projections and expectations in your story is a wonderful way to wake up to the information that you give away in your life. As you live into your story and begin living into your life in a more conscious way, keep your eyes and heart open to other places where you may give away your information. Recognizing information as "your information" is an important part of living into the story that you are creating. Focusing outward as you engage is how a lot of information can get lost. In the same way that the projection and expectation of information can subtly distract you, so can focusing your own information outward. By focusing your attention outward you may miss situations your heart has called in to help you move through your old information.

As you are learning, you can only engage in your life and your story, not others' lives and stories. Well, let's take this concept a step further. If you find yourself in a situation with a person where there is conflict, or you feel that there is an emotional hiccup, that is a signal to focus inward and find the information for yourself. If you find yourself in an environment where you feel out of sorts or struggling, that is a signal to turn your focus inward and find the information that your heart is calling in for you. For most people this is a totally new perspective. In the end, however, this single shift in perspective can help you find harmony with yourself. Recognizing and focusing inward on your information is a tool that can help you live in a more downstream and harmonizing way.

It's easy to get into an argument with someone and focus on how wrong they are or how at fault they are. By focusing your attention on the person you are arguing with, you can overlook what the argument is there to show you and teach you. There is probably information surrounding the argument that your heart called in so that you could lift up old piles of information. Someone may cut you off on the drive home and your immediate reaction is to yell at them for cutting you off. You feel yourself getting (even if it's for a moment) worked up about what they could have done to you or how stupid they are. If your focus is on them, then you can miss the information that might be there for you. You may say that you were minding your own business, and it was their stupidity that almost smacked you in the face. Looking at it differently, you could also say that the problem is less about them and more about you. How did you get to the place where you were almost smacked in the face? What about that situation really bothered you? What is the information that feels like the hiccup? Can you put words around it for yourself? It's that kind of engagement and curiosity that helps you begin to turn your focus inward. Inward is where you find the juicy information that can create the shift in your life that you may need to move forward in your story.

Being in an argument may elicit the same kind of outward-reaching reaction. Any argument you engage in is less about the other person than it is about you. If this is your life and you can only live your life, then logically the argument has to be more about you. The minute you focus outside, you have lost the opportunity to learn the lesson and move though the information that is yours. Don't worry, your heart will keep calling in the information that it needs to lift up the old information until you pay attention.

Max's Story

LET'S WALK THROUGH A SITUATION THAT MAX found himself in to illustrate what it can look like to recognize and engage in your own information. Max is a man who was making an effort to own the information that had come up in his life more and more frequently. He had experienced some major losses that brought him to a place where he felt like he was not in control. This perceived loss of control motivated him to wake up to his story. He had been slowly trying to recognize and engage in the situations around him as if they had been created especially for him. He felt a little silly framing his experience in this way at first. The perspective felt off, as if by looking inward he was being selfish somehow. However, the more he took in, the more he saw that it was less about being selfish and more about being engaged. He had not realized just how asleep he had been. He had not felt asleep until he began to wake up, "rubbed his eyes," and saw things in a new way. Once he was able to let go of the initial awkwardness, he found that each time he moved though situations and information as if they were there for him, it got easier to see how they applied to his story.

A little background on Max might be helpful so you can understand how he was able to recognize and claim his information as his own. Max had spent his twenties finishing up college and establishing himself in the business communication world. He had a job that felt secure, in a company that he believed in. The job never quite fulfilled his creative side, so he often found himself writing short stories or songs on the guitar. It was how he kept himself balanced. Not many people even knew that his happiest evenings were spent coming up with stories about love, life, and loss. When he lost the grandparents who had practically raised him, he felt that any sense of control or balance had been nothing but a joke. With them gone, he didn't want to live out another decade in a life where the things that made him the happiest were only done a couple hours out of the week. Every time he thought about how much he loved his grandparents, he could not help but be reminded that he had to fully engage in the things that he loved. There was not one thing left unsaid between the three of them, but life is almost always shorter than we think. He was about to enter his thirties and he wanted to take advantage of the fact that he knew what brought him joy. As much as he wanted it for himself, it was also what his grandparents would have wanted for him. This leads us to the circumstance where Max was able to shift his perspective inward and own his information.

Max was involved in community projects and regularly worked on events that brought art and music to his city. He enjoyed being around creative people and found collaboration beneficial to his own creativity. He had been working with a wonderful group of people to create an event that they hoped would raise awareness of how important the arts were in education. His assignment had been to arrange the music for the event, and he had put together a lineup that he was happy with. There were still a few holes to fill, but he had some ideas on the direction he wanted to go.

It was under this set of circumstances that Max's opportunity to recognize and claim his information emerged. Max met and talked with a great guitar player who had been creating some wonderful and cutting-edge new work. The musician's work started with a story, and by using new technology and his guitar, he was able to communicate all the characters differently in the story. He was creating beautiful music while he told an incredible story. Max loved this musician's process and the music itself was awesome. They talked about the event and what a perfect fit it would be to have him perform. They both agreed and exchanged information. Max left the party feeling like he had called in some great information. He reflected on how brilliant it was that they were both, in their own way, storytellers.

He made contact with the musician by email first, just to say how wonderful it was to meet him, and gave him the date of the event along with the other information. The musician responded and let him know that he was interested, and that he would get back to him to verify that he would be able to commit. A week later Max followed up with a voicemail, but days later the musician had still not communicated his commitment—Max was beginning to get frustrated. He kept thinking *follow up already*. He could not believe the musician was not following through. They had had such a great conversation and this felt like a betrayal to Max. The frustration Max felt gave him the clue to look at the situation a little closer, to look at it from his new perspective instead of being angry at his colleague.

He wondered if he was giving some sort of information away. Max recognized that he needed to turn the focus of the information inward if he was going to be able to use it for himself. The outward feeling was frustration because the guy was not following through. If he looked inward and took the information as his own, then he needed to see where in his story he was not following though. Max's feelings were not about the event. He had been crossing every *t* and dotting every *i*. He got quiet and curious with his story, and in that place he could see the message clearly. The information was for him. He had not followed through with his writing. He had wanted to join a writers' group and maybe even take an evening class. The paperwork had been sitting on his kitchen table for weeks now. He even had emails about the group sitting in his inbox. The coincidence was too obvious; it was as if the story that is his life was linked up with everything around him. He had not noticed just how connected all the information actually was. Could it really be that his heart was calling this circumstance in so that he would follow through with what he had, after all, been wanting? All of the people and circumstances that he could have easily shrugged off were like notations on the road map of his story. He wondered if it could really be that easy to claim your information. "It's less about them and more about me." The simple but challenging concept had worked its magic. Once he realized that he needed to turn his perspective inward, he could recognize the information as his and use it to help him harmonize his heart.

Max was able to let go of the frustration he had been feeling toward the musician and appreciate the information for what it was. He also let go of the expectations that he had placed on the musician and realized that he didn't want to fight to make it happen. It would be great to have him be a part of the event, but Max knew that he could fill the spot with someone else if he needed to. Because he used the information to help him move forward in his own story, it became less about the musician anyway. As it turned out, once Max used the information as his own and started to follow through with his own story by signing up for his class and the writing group, his heart knew that he was listening and he was able to call in different information.

Had Max not turned his focus inward, his heart might have had to call in the information in a louder way. When you are not paying attention to the information, your heart will continue to call circumstances in to help you pay attention to what it is trying to shift. As the circumstances build, it is as if your heart is turning the volume up so that you pay attention. As you recognize and claim the information that comes into your life, remember to be tender with yourself. As you engage with tender curiosity, your heart will know that you are paying attention to both the new and the old information. You may begin to notice that the new information that comes in does so more gently.

Tabitha's and Max's stories embodied the essence of living only your life. They each began by awakening to their stories, and as they continued to awaken, they were able to step into the truth of living their own lives. They were able move through the distractions of other people's information and the need to control them. They were also able to let go of expectations that they had for others as well as themselves. All of this helped build a new perspective and relationship with the information in their stories.

CHAPTER 3

It's All Just Information

⌇⌇⌇

B Y NOW, YOU ARE BEGINNING TO SEE that there is a myriad of information around you and the impact it has on your existence is enormous. You have been able to see how the information unfolded as Avery, William, Tabitha, and Max awakened to, and engaged more in, the story of their lives. Everything that you are conscious of is your information. So often, we dismiss or give away our information. The ideas, methods, and principles in this book, and how they play and work together, are all based on seeing and engaging with your information. You can train your mind and heart to look inward and notice the information that you have called in. This is one of the keys to unlocking harmony within your story. Whether it is loud and obtrusive, or gentle and subtle, the information is yours. As you begin to understand the nuances and importance of your information and acknowledge it, you are also going to look at how you respond to it once you have sight of it. Then as you ground yourself and settle into claiming it, you will learn how to interact with the information that you pull from the situations in your life.

The three areas that you will be exploring are:

1) Acknowledging your information.

2) Understanding how you respond to your information.

3) Learning how to interact with your information.

Acknowledging Your Information

ACKNOWLEDGING YOUR INFORMATION TAKES CURIOSITY, honesty, and a little bit of bravery. With curiosity you have the openness to look inward. The honesty allows you see what is actually yours, while the bravery gives you ability to claim it. Curiosity is invaluable because it gets you engaged in the picture, but if you do not have the ability to be honest with yourself, there is little need for bravery.

Being honest with yourself can be challenging. This is where some people get stuck. If you don't have a good, established relationship with the inner part of yourself, then you may find it hard to be honest as you acknowledge the information that belongs to you. There may be too many inner voices distracting or pulling your attention away from what is honestly your information. "Can you believe what they did to me or what is happening to me?" There may also be too much projected judgment to get through to the information. "If this information belongs to me, then I am a bad person, and/or I am wrong for feeling this way." Try to take out the judgment by embracing the idea that it is all just information. If the information is neutral, not good or bad, neither right nor wrong, then there is no room for judgment. If it is all just information, then there is no reason to hide from it, either. This idea can also quiet the inner voices that may distract you from seeing what is meant for you.

When you are able to look honestly at the situations that come up in your everyday life, you will begin to notice what information is important to you in the position you have come to in your story. Acknowledging your information becomes a precious resource. Turning your perspective inward and acknowledging your information as your own is like looking through the lens of a camera. When you recognize as yours the information in a situation, you have the ability to adjust the lens. If the situation feel like it's too big, too much, or too cluttered, then you can pull back and take note that it is a small portion of a bigger picture. That acknowledgement also allows you to zoom in on areas that resonate with you and allows you to see them without the noise and distraction that may have been in your initial snapshot of the situation.

Once you are able to look at your information from a place of honesty, the bravery comes into play. As you set your lens on the information—the picture that you are looking at—it becomes fully your own. You have shifted the perspective and claimed it as your information. Being able to step up to the information and own it can be unnerving. It may go against old patterns of thinking, but as you live into the knowledge that it is there for you, it becomes worth the effort and discomfort it took to shift the perspective. As you acknowledge your information as your own, you find yourself more conscious and engaged in your story.

A good indicator that you are acknowledging your information is when you can say to yourself, "This situation is less about the other person or the situation and more about me." This statement does not come from a place of ego. The statement "it is less about them and more about me" is not an externally projected statement where you find yourself climbing over someone else for value or importance. This is an inward, heart-centered exchange that is there to help you focus on and determine what information belongs to you and what information belongs to someone else and remains unchangeable. It is a strong, yet gentle, statement that, if used correctly, can lead to harmony and balance within your heart and story. This allows the information to direct you to a place where you can find understanding and connection within. As you claim your information and connect to its purpose, you will be able to uncover the old information that may be acting as a barrier to the harmony that you are longing for.

Recognizing How You Respond to Your Information

Now that you have claimed your information, it is important to recognize how you respond to it. Recognizing how you respond to your information will help you understand where you are in relationship to the information that you are acknowledging. Recognizing and not recognizing how you interact with the information is like the contrast between navigating a lit hallway versus a dark one. You can make it down a dark hallway, but it's significantly easier if there is a light on. If you know how you naturally respond to or process your information, then it is easier to move through it, just as it is easier to move through a lit hallway. This recognition can make it easier for you as you begin to navigate through your information.

For some people, their natural first response to information is to see it and hold it at a safe distance away from them. For others, the response may be to control it. Another kind of person likes to take it all in and hibernate with it, so that they can understand all of the nuances within it. Still others find that they respond to their information by outwardly expressing what it is that they are learning. Some people need to do the same thing over and over again to make sure that they can trust themselves with information. As you can see, people respond to information in myriad ways. To find your response style, think back on a big important situation that happened within your story. Births, deaths, loves, breakups, new adventures, and plans; when these things first crossed the threshold of your story, how did you respond to them? See if you can remember if you sat and absorbed the situation within yourself or ran to find the first person you could tell before you even began to process it. This will help you understand how you respond to information.

In responding to the information, you have two options: You can react to it or interact with it. One of benefits of living into your story and becoming more conscious is that rather than having a forced reaction to the information, you get the opportunity to have a voluntary interaction with it instead. While this shift takes place, you may still find yourself responding to your information in the same way that you always have. If you process inwardly and like to hibernate with your information, then you may still respond to it in the same way. The difference is that instead of having your mind and heart *react* to whatever the information is, you will be able to *interact* with it instead. If you happen to be a person who finds yourself responding to the information by running out to communicate with people about what is going on, then you may still run out and find people to digest the information with. However, rather than reacting to the inner working of the information as you outwardly talk about it, you will find yourself interacting with the information at hand as you talk with the people you sought out. No matter what your response to the information, interacting with it will bring awareness instead of the upheaval that happens when you react to it.

Whether you respond inwardly or outwardly, shutting down to your information is one of the hidden ways of reacting to it. Understanding how you respond can help you create a space that will allow you to stay open to your information. If you are an inward interactor, you may find it helpful to leave yourself extra room so that you feel safe enough to engage with the information. Zoom the lens of the camera out so that you see a bigger part of the picture. This will give you enough perspective so that you don't get so frightened that you shut down and can't engage.

If you find yourself processing and responding externally, then you may want to narrow the focus and look at the finer details. This will keep your dialogue clean and keep you from getting lost in the information that does not belong to you. This will also allow you to create a more internal perspective that might otherwise get lost if you work more externally with your information. The beautiful part of this process is that, even if you do shut down, the shutting down itself is just information. Once you can see the act of shutting down as your own, you can pick that information up, use the principles to help you navigate through it, and find the release that your heart has been looking for.

Learning How to Interact With Your Information

INTERACTING WITH YOUR INFORMATION IS JUST THAT, interacting with it. You can create an atmosphere in which you interact with the information in your life rather than reacting to it, or feel like it has bombarded you. The information comes in, and a reciprocal exchange is triggered. Circumstances don't just happen to you. By interacting with the information, you are able to have an influence on how situations affect you, and you get to take a more active role in what is coming into your story and life. When interacting with your information, you get to create an internal dialogue that allows you to feel completely engaged in your story. Once you felt controlled or drained by everyday situations. When you interact with them as information, you can find purpose, power, and a wellspring of energy that moves you forward. Interacting with your information allows you to break down what is coming into your life and use it to help you find peace, connection, joy, or whatever it is your heart truly longs for. As this happens, you allow the incoming information to fulfill its purpose, completing that reciprocal exchange. The information comes in, you engage with it, and it serves its purpose. It can then move out instead of cluttering your psyche by adding itself to the piles of old information around you. In fact, new information moving out can also shift, and take with it some of those old piles that are lying around.

As you start to break down the information that comes in, you must be curious and turn your perspective inward to find its purpose and utilize it. Have you ever felt like you know a lot about the information around you, but you don't know how to get beyond it? As you acknowledge and interact with the information, it helps you find and understand its purpose and then you can move beyond it. No matter how big or small, how positive or negative a situation may feel at first, when it has purpose within your story, it can be seen as a valuable gift.

Now let's look at some self-talk that may help you create the interaction we have been discussing. These statements will help you stay true to your information as well as guide you along the right track. The first one we have already touched on, but it is the most valuable, so it's worth restating. "It's less about the situation and more about me." You can add to that statement these others that promote interaction: "It is just information." "Slow down and be curious and tender." "My heart is ready." You can use these like mantras to help keep you focused as you are navigating through your information. As you go through the deeper meaning of each mantra, you will notice how they work together.

It's Less About the Situation and More About Me

IT'S LESS ABOUT THE SITUATION AND MORE ABOUT ME: As you repeat this statement to yourself, remember to say it, not as a loud ego-driven statement, but as a quiet heart-driven statement. "It's less about the situation and more about me." The statement helps you create a separation between the information that is yours and what belongs to someone else. If it is your information, you can respond to it and interact with it productively, but if it belongs to someone else, you won't ever really be able to move through it. You can try, but in the end the attempt at movement will just not be productive. When you are tangled up in the emotion and energy of a situation with another person, it can feel as if it has to be about them. You focus on other people because they are the ones calling everything up in your heart and mind. Your mind keeps going to them and what it is that they are creating within you. The emotions may be

good or they may be fraught with negativity. If you can use this statement to try to cut the cords that tether you to other people or situations,
you will be able to find some perspective. "It is less about you and more
about me." Once you have some space created between you and the other
person, you will be able to get to the core of why your heart calls the
situation in. You will be able to ask: what is it about the situation that is
affecting me so much? What old information is my heart really tethered
to? If it is less about them and more about me, then where am I feeling
this the most? When you are able to find the essence behind the situation
and give it purpose, then you can use that momentum to move beyond
the limited or wounded place within your heart that is holding on to all
the old information.

This statement will also help you recognize that there is a difference
between the information and the vehicle that it comes to you in. This creates a subtle variation in statement by expanding your attention to include
the difference between the person you're interacting with and the information that they happen to be bringing up within you. This is important for
two reasons: The first is that this differentiation helps you get deeper into
the information; and the second is that your reaction is a perfect indicator,
showing you if you have truly harmonized with and moved through the
old wound in your heart.

When you are wrapped up in drama or emotionally tethered by a situation, you have a hard time seeing the difference between the person and
the information that they are calling up in you. You may be able to see that
it is less about them and more about you, but you still remain a bit stuck.
If this happens, take the statement a step deeper and notice the difference
between the person and the information. Try to take the person out of the
equation and just sit with the information that remains. Once the other
person is filtered out, you are left with the information that your heart
wanted you to navigate through.

Once you have navigated through the information, you can use the
statement as an indicator to see where your heart stands. If the old wound
is cleared and you have navigated your way through the information to
find a place of harmony, then you will be able to interact with the person
again from a neutral place. You may even be able to interact from a deeper
place of love and gratitude. The person acts as your mirror, and what you

create together allows you to uncover parts of your heart that you might not have been able to see without that interaction. If you interact again from a shifted place, you will be able to feel that the tangled frustration is gone, because it was less about the other person and more about you. When you shift the information for yourself, you allow the person you are in conflict with to just be who they happen to be. The other person may still be frustrating or tangled, but you will notice that you no longer interact in that limited way—you no longer get drawn into that part of the dialogue. Laws of attraction say, where you (your mind and heart) are determine what you will draw in. If your heart is shifted, then what you will draw in will mirror that shifted place. The next time you interact, that person may mirror the shift that you created within your own heart.

It Is Just Information

THIS STATEMENT WORKS OFF OF, AND PLAYS INTO, the first statement. It helps neutralize frustration, anxiety, and tension. It can also help to take the sting out of some potent or painful situations. It helps you broaden the lens and see the bigger picture. As humans, we are easily lost or swept up in the events around us. Sometimes it's fun to get a little lost, but if you end up lost or struggling, then this statement will help you to find your way back.

When you pair this statement with the understanding that your heart calls in the information that you need to shift and evolve beyond the old wounded information, then you find strength within yourself and your story. If your heart has called it in, and if it is all just information, then nothing can possibly be too big for you to navigate though. If you are able to look at it as the information that it is, then you can handle anything that pops up in your story.

It is important to remember that your heart is behind the information. By using the statement, "It is all just information," you can bring yourself back into a more neutral place, making it easier to interact with your information. The statement is not intended to make you numb or lose touch with your emotions. You don't want to rob yourself of the experience of the feelings behind the information. Remember, you create contrast for yourself so that you can create movement. Often that contrast manifests itself not only in your physical interactions but your emotional ones as well. When the pendulum has swung to one side and the contrast is blatant, the contrast may have clouded your ability to consciously engage because your emotions or feelings are heightened. This statement will help you swing the pendulum back in the other direction so that you can navigate through the information that brought you to this point. The trick is not over-analyzing the experience, but finding the balance of feeling the emotion behind the situation and using it to move you forward. You want to be able to linger in each phase of the information for as long as you need to, which leads us logically into the next statement.

Slow Down and Be Curious and Tender

THIS IS YOUR STORY AND EVERYTHING that comes into your life is your information. There are no timelines or pressures unless you accept them as part of your story. As you begin to feel your way through each phase of the navigation process, you need to remember to take your time and be tender with yourself. The statement "Slow down and be curious and tender" will help to remind you. This is your brilliant story, and you have all the time you need to live into it. Stay in each phase until you are truly done with it. Passing over information is just fine. Sometimes you'll feel like you don't have it in you to work your way through it. This is where the tenderness part comes into play. Just be tender with your heart. If you can't get to the bottom of the information at a particular point in time, know that it will eventually come to you in a way that you can. You need to keep in mind that when you pass over information with the intention to come back to it and you don't, your heart will call in louder information that will be harder to turn away from. The volume at which your information comes in is relative to how you process your information. If you listen and move through the information as you see it coming in, your heart will know that you are paying attention. The volume of the information will be dialed down, and you will see that it gets more and more gentle. If you are not paying attention to your heart and keep pushing your information back or ignoring it, the volume will get louder and louder until you must pay attention. This is where you find the greatest contrast. Your heart knows how you interact with your information and exactly what it is you need to pay attention to.

As your heart calls in the information that you need to pay attention to, your next goal is to become curious as in comes in. Tenderly ask yourself questions that start to turn your perspective inward. You can begin with some of the questions we talked about earlier.

- ❧ What is it about the situation that is affecting me so much?
- ❧ What old information is it that my heart is really tethered to?
- ❧ If it is less about them and more about me, then where is it that my heart feels it the most?
- ❧ Have I felt this before?
- ❧ When was the first time I felt it?
- ❧ Where do I feel it in my body?
- ❧ Is it in my throat, dealing with my voice?
- ❧ Is it in my chest, dealing with my heart?
- ❧ Is it in my stomach, dealing with my need for protection or security?

The questions can be endless and, as long as they focus you inward, you are headed in the right direction. This leads us to the last statement.

My Heart Is Ready

As you tenderly ask yourself the questions that focus you on the information that your heart called in, realize that if your heart was not ready to shift and create movement you would not be where you are. Making the statement "My heart is ready" may come in handy. Have you ever caught yourself saying that you are *so over* something, or that you are *so done* with this? You try to put it down because you are over it, but inevitably you find yourself engaging in it moments later. If you find yourself saying things like this, then your heart is ready, but you have to create movement to go beyond that wounded place. You call in the situation that leads you to the feeling that you were *so done*. You call it in because your heart is ready to move beyond it. It no longer wants to hold on to the old wound. It no longer wants the new information to be filtered through the piles of old information. It is ready for the present information that comes into your story to be just that, present information. Know that your heart is ready, and navigate your way through the information.

These statements are just the beginning. As you use them, you will find yourself becoming more consciously engaged in your story. This allows you to open up to all of the information that is around you, and inevitably leads you to finding harmony within your heart. Understanding that everything that comes into your life can be used as your information will help create a neutral space of learning where you learn to interact rather than react. As you acknowledge your information, settle in to how you respond to it, and then interact with it, you create endless possibilities for your own happiness and connection. It is all your information, so you might as well use it for all that it's worth, because its worth is priceless.

Living into the Change

❧❧❧

L ET'S TALK ABOUT YOU. You will find yourself "Awakening to Your Story" as you practice the unique techniques and use the powerful tools in this book. While your perspective changes, your relationship with the information within your story will continue to grow stronger. You will find yourself curiously looking for your information and feeling the relief of giving back information that doesn't really belong to you. As you awaken and live more completely into your life, you will need some practical ways to stay engaged with the valuable information that you uncover.

Part Two of *Awakening to Your Story* is all about living into a change in perspective that you have created for yourself. You will be introduced to tools that can help you embody this change. You will also learn how to use these powerful tools, giving you the ability to shift, create, and live the life of positive change that your heart desires.

The practical approach of using "mirrors" and "reflections" is introduced as an aid to identifying information within circumstances and situations that come up in your life. You will also be introduced to and learn how to incorporate the Stream-Kayak Principle into your everyday life. Along with these tools, you will also receive instruction on how to give purpose to the patterns, voices, and scenarios that play out in your mind and within your story.

These tools will allow you to live into a change in perspective that you have created for yourself. You will be able to effectively identify and navigate through your own information. The second part of *Awakening to Your Story* reveals unique techniques that can strengthen your power to interact with life's challenges and actively live the life of positive change that you desire.

CHAPTER 4

Mirrors and Reflections

⌒⌒⌒⌒

Tabitha's and Max's stories showed you how you can recognize your own information in situations where you might not normally look for it. By turning your perspective inward, you can uncover the information that is right there, ready to help you. Whether your reason for awakening to your story is because you want to find an inner happiness, or you are just tired of struggling, your heart is behind it. No matter what brought you to this place, your heart is at the center of the story.

Your heart calls in the information that it needs to heal old wounds. It calls in the interactions that it needs to help you move through the piles of old information that you have been carrying around with you. There is a part of you that longs to be connected and moving through your life in perfect harmony with everything around you. Your heart calls in the information that it needs to get you to that place. Your job is to engage with that information in the best way that you can, with integrity of the heart. I love this concept—integrity of the heart. It is a position from which you can use everything that you know from the relationship that you have with your heart and your story. You use what is true to your heart at that moment, in that capacity, with honesty and inward compassion.

As you live into your story with integrity of the heart, you open yourself up to a place where you can more easily claim and use your information to heal and harmonize your heart. Once you have settled into that new space within your story, you can fully begin to search out your information. One of the most effective ways of finding your information is by using all the people around you and situations you find yourself in as mirrors to reflect the inner whispers of your heart. There may be an old pile of information that your heart is ready to shift. Your heart then calls in information that you can use to move through that shift. Your heart might be tired of carrying that information around with you every day. Maybe you have learned all you need to learn from the place where a wound was created, and now your heart is ready to heal, so your capacity can expand beyond the lessons that you have learned. Your heart wants to find harmony, and by using all of the mirrors and reflections that surround you, it's possible for you to find that harmony more effectively.

Let's think about how mirrors and reflections serve us in everyday life. When you brush your hair in the morning, most of you use a mirror so that you can see if you are effectively achieving the task at hand. You can see if your part is the way you like it or if everything is laying the way you want. Of course you can brush your hair without the mirror, but you may not be able to see that there is a large chunk of hair matted in the back or sticking out on the side—but you can get the job done. On the other hand, when you look at your reflection in a mirror, you can more easily perceive the full information about your hair. You can address the tangles and straighten out the hair that was going crazy. You may be able to put on your makeup or shave your face without a mirror as well, but it's easier and more effective when you use the mirror as a tool.

Just as you use a mirror to help you get information about your body and surroundings, you can use a mirror to help you see the inner workings of your heart. It's a little bit more challenging to train your mind to see the reflections of your heart than it is to train your eyes to see the reflections of the space around you. When, as a baby, you see your reflection for the first time, you don't understand that what you're seeing is *you.* You think you are seeing someone else. Once you reach self-awareness, you comprehend the concept of the mirror, and understand that you are seeing a reflection of yourself. In a similar way when you begin looking at the information around you using a mirror, you first must train yourself to understand that the information is your own and not someone else's. With some time and attention, your mind and your heart will be able to see these brilliant reflections all around you. Just as it's easier to comb your hair in front of a mirror, you will find that it is easier to navigate situations that your heart calls in when you look at them through a mirror. These reflections will also allow you to see your heart's information more clearly, so that you can navigate through it more effectively.

If you look at the information that comes into your daily life as a refection of something within, you can see more clearly what your heart needs. Then, if the information comes in as a hiccup, you can navigate through it to a place where you no longer need the old information that it is reflecting. If the situation is mirroring something positive, you can bask in the beauty of it and gather up more positive cellular memories. The more you find yourself accepting your heart and your story, the more your heart will call in mirrors of joy, peace, happiness, and the positive things that tickle your heart.

Your heart's mirrors are always around you. Some reflect the enlightened parts of your heart, and others reflect the challenged parts of your heart. When you claim the information as yours, it is as if you turn on the light so you can begin to see the reflection in those mirrors. Once you can see them, you can identify what the information is, and from there you can begin to navigate through it. The information is there for you to use; your heart has called it in, and it's up to you to step farther into your story to navigate and clear through the old information. Stepping more into your story and consciousness will allow your heart to move through the old piles of information and allow you to clear through some of the things that are blocking you from feeling truly fulfilled and engaged in your happiness.

Let's look at how you can start to shift to an inward perspective of your story by using mirrors and reflections as your tool. The first step is to look. This means stepping up to the information mirrored for you and really looking at it with curiosity. The second step is identifying what part of the situation is your mirror. The third step is connecting to the old information that wants to be shifted. The fourth and final step is turning inward, giving yourself the space to engage with the information and the action it takes to shift through the old information.

1) *Look* – Step up to the mirror and look at the refection.
2) *Identify* – Identify why and how it's your mirror.
3) *Recognize* – Connect to the old information or the wound that is associated with it.
4) *Engage* – Engage with and shift that old information.

Let's take a look at each step a little closer so you can see how it works:

Step Up and Look

WHEN YOU USE A PHYSICAL MIRROR to brush your hair, you step up to the mirror and take a look at yourself and then proceed to brush your hair. The first step in using information as your heart's mirror is the same. You can step up to the mirror, but unless you truly look at what is in it, you won't be able to see what the information holds. It takes curiosity to look into the mirrors that are around you. Seeing the information might take a little courage and honesty. Looking for the information and seeing the information tend to be different things. Sometimes when a situation has arisen, we can tell there is information in it for us, but when we look into it as a mirror, we can't quite find the reflection of our heart. This leads us to step two.

Identify the Mirror and Statement

THE SECOND STEP IS IDENTIFYING how the information in the mirror is your reflection. There is usually a statement that you can extract from the situation that narrows the complexities down to their essence. This is where the difference in looking and seeing the information comes into play. When you finally see the information for what it is, and can claim it, then you can use it to connect with the old information that is ready to be shifted. This leads us directly into step three.

Learn How to Interact With the Information

HERE, YOU MUST RECOGNIZE why you have called in the situation as a mirror. By truly seeing the reflection in the mirror, you can find the link to the old information. Identifying the old information that your heart is calling up allows you to create a new relationship with it. As you engage the old information through the mirror, you are changing your relationship to it. Rather than reacting to the situation or filtering it through the old information, you are engaging with it as exactly what it is, *information*. It's a very different and powerful position. With the space that you create by recognizing information, you can grow closer to your own personal freedom and connection with your heart. From there you can move on to step four.

Engage With and Shift the Old Information

IN THIS STEP YOU TURN INWARD AND ENGAGE the information. This may manifest itself in a variety of ways. You may work with the information and find a way to shift your heart so that the old information no longer holds the space that it once did. You may engage with the information as an indicator of where you are in your story and heart. The mirror may be showing you how far you have come or how far you have to go until the wound that was created by the old information is completely healed. You may find that engaging with the information takes on the look of an exercise that your heart wants you to walk through so that you can slowly navigate through the old information with clarity and certainty. The information can, at times, be challenging to fully engage with, and the exercises that naturally may come from the information can be a little challenging as well. It is important to know that your heart is up to the challenge and that if it called the information in, then it is ready to let go and grow beyond the limitations that it was being bound by.

Chloe's Story: Look, Identify, Recognize, Engage

NOW THAT YOU HAVE LOOKED AT THE INDIVIDUAL STEPS, let's look at an illustration of what walking through those steps can look like. I want to introduce you to Chloe. Before we start looking into one of situations she found as a mirror for her heart, let's delve into Chloe's backstory. Chloe is a woman whose greatest desire is to be married and create a family. She lives a full life. She works for an advertising company, and in her spare time reviews music for a local magazine. Her family lives close by and she loves spending time with her nephews. If she had created a to-do list for her life ten years ago, she would be able to cross most of those things off that list today. The only two things that would be left would be getting married and starting a family. If, before she awakened to her story, you had asked her about her previous relationships, she would have gone into a long rant about how unsuccessful they were. You would have gotten an earful about how challenged these guys were, how they couldn't really engage with her and always kept her at arm's distance, far from where she wanted to be in the relationship. Now that she is settled into her story more, she might tell you that she had called useful information in through her prior relationships. Chloe has successfully begun turning her perspective inward and has uncovered some wonderful information about why she is where she is in her life. She has been able to see why she called in the men she did. She also recognizes that, as she began shifting her heart-space, the men and mirrors that she had been calling in were significantly shifting as well.

This brings us to a Tuesday in the spring. Chloe had been sitting in the waiting room of her doctor's office. The door opened and a very attractive man walked through it. She found herself sitting up a little bit taller. She tried to focus on the magazine in her lap, but her eyes kept finding their way back to him. She could hear him talking to the woman at the reception desk. From what she could tell, he was a firefighter and had injured his leg somehow. From the way he was standing, she couldn't tell which leg was hurt. She found herself wondering how he had gotten hurt. He took a seat a couple of chairs down from her and began to fill out paperwork. This was perfect. She could study him without him noticing. He had a couple of tattoos that she could see peeking out on his arm from under his T-shirt. She loved tattoos on a man. She had not been able to catch a glimpse of his ring finger yet to tell if he was married. As she waited for the finger to present itself, she noticed the laugh lines around his eyes and the freckles that you could hardly see on his tanned face. He was very attractive to her and all she needed was to see if he was married. Just as the thought popped up in her mind again, he checked his watch and flashed the gold band around his ring finger. Damn, she thought to herself, so close. She sent a text to one of her girlfriends explaining just how attracted she was to this man in the waiting room. "I am so close, just look at what I can manifest for myself. Now if I can just get that ring to not be there."

The nurse called her name and she went back into the room. By the time she came back out, he was nowhere to be seen. She kept thinking about just how cute he was and that silly ring. "What a great reminder," she thought to herself. "They are out there." This was a refreshing approach to the information. Usually, she would have focused on how all the good ones were taken, but today she felt lucky to know that they are out there.

Chloe had stepped up to the mirror and was looking at all the information. She felt excited that there was an indicator in the mirror showing her that she had been able to change her pessimistic perspective to one full of optimism. She basked in that information. The interaction was an indicator of just how far along she had come. Without it, she might not have been able to see that milestone within her story. As the day pressed on, she realized that she had kept replaying the image of the ring on his finger. She wondered if she had used all of the information from that situation. If it kept playing over and over again, maybe her heart saw more information there for her. Had she really looked into the mirror and seen the true reflection of the information her heart needed?

"There must be a reason that I keep coming back to the ring. What is it about that ring? There is a part of my heart that the ring is reflecting back to me," she thought. She gently sat with curiosity as she tried to be very honest with herself. "Sitting in front of me was a man that I was super attracted to and because he was married I couldn't actually engage with him in the way that I would have liked. I can't engage with him," she thought. "That's interesting. That sounds like the reverse of the tagline from my last four relationships." She had navigated through some of the old boyfriend information before, so she was familiar with some of the information that was coming up. "In each of my past relationships, the guys couldn't or wouldn't engage fully with me." Each relationship had, however, mirrored the progression that she had experienced within her own story. With each one, she seemed to get a little closer to the connection that she longed for, but that separation from truly being able to engage fully still seemed to be there.

"Now, here I am with the same information, just given to me in a little bit different way. The ring is mirroring back that separation. I am calling in, and am attracted to, men who do not have the capacity to connect fully. If I am honest with myself," she thought, "in some way the separation feels safe or comfortable to me. How interesting," she wondered. "I must be getting closer if all it takes to get the information is running into a guy at the doctor's office. This mirroring is far more gentle than investing in yet another relationship that leaves me completely empty."

Chloe's outward longing to feel connected in a relationship is what her heart truly wants, while her heart's inward longing is to move through the old information so that she has the freedom to actually be connected. The outward longing and inward longing are working together to get her to where she ultimately wants to go. At this point, she is filtering her new information through the old piles of information. Her heart is calling in the information that she needs to clear it out, and as she engages with it, the layers of old information begin to lift. This leaves her a little bit closer to connecting in the way that she has been longing for. As she connects to her story and her heart, she is also living into the experience of true union. As she connects with herself, her capacity for true bonding deepens and grows, enabling her to outwardly find that place of connection with another human.

"The old information has something to do with feeling safer or more comfortable interacting with people when I can always be a little separated from full connection and love," Chloe realized. "When did that information start?" she asked herself. She knew that she could not have come into this world with that limitation. It was something that she had gathered. It was information that someone else had given to her. She looked into her heart and knew exactly where the information had come from. It was interesting, she had been working on this same pile of information layer by layer. She really thought she had moved through it completely. A little disappointed, she remembered that the information was called in more gently this time than the last. This realization made her feel more hopeful and ready to look at the next layer of information she had gathered from her relationship with her father.

She saw herself sitting at the far end of the dinner table. She was so excited to tell her father about the day that she had, but every time she started in on her story, her father would interrupt her and carry on with his own conversation. After dinner, she tried again to talk with him. She tiptoed into his study and snuck up behind the chair he was sitting in. "Daddy," her little voice broke through the silence of the room. "Not now sweetie," his voice replied. "I am very busy, and I have to get through all this paperwork tonight." She remembers putting her head down and climbing into the wingback chair in the corner of his office, where she fell asleep. She woke up in her bed the next morning, and her father was already at work. This was where the old information of separation from connection had started.

At this point, Chloe has stepped up and looked at the mirrors that the situation gave to her, step one. She has then identified her information by seeing indicators in the reflection, step two. When she looked a little deeper at the information in the mirror, she was able to find how she could connect the new information that she called in with the mirror to a pile of old information. This action was a combination of steps two and three. As she acknowledged that her heart had called it in, she moved toward step four where she turned the information inward and worked toward engaging with it and shifting the old information to a place where she no longer needs it. As Chloe engages further in step four, she can clear away the old information that is blocking her. Let's continue to see how she follows through with the mirror that this situation created.

"So it looks as if I am still calling in, or am attracted to, men who have little or no capacity to connect with me in the way that I would like them to," Chloe thought. "This so perfectly mirrors the old information that my interactions are filtering through." She is always a little surprised when she uncovers the old information and sees how brilliantly it has been mirrored through the new information. "My relationship with the first man that I created love and connection with was one where there was always separation. No wonder that is what is comfortable to me. I keep calling in men who can't engage with me fully because my old information says that's what is comfortable, but there is a part of my heart that is still that girl who is excited to share and wants to engage," Chloe thinks.

From here, Chloe is looking at and tenderly identifying with the old information. Now she needs to turn what she has found inward. Because this is her story, it's less about the men she has been calling in and it's less about her dad—it's more about her. Her dad gave to her and interacted with her, using the capacity that he had at the time. It's painful when someone's capacity does not meet your needs. Often, this is where a wound may be created. However, when you turn inward and give yourself space to engage with your old information from your current position as the conscious adult that you are today, you can heal that wound.

"It's not about my dad. It's less about my dad and more about me," she repeats to herself. If it's less about my dad and it's more about me, then I can move through the information. If I make it about my dad, then it's impossible to create movement because I can't know or shift his information for him. I can, however, know and shift my information," she reminds herself.

Because this is about Chloe, and the information is hers to use, she can now go into the place where the wound was created and create the space to heal that wounded and separated part within her. She is able to do this by looking to see what it is that the girl sitting in the wingback chair, or at the dinner table, needed. After all, she is the only one who really knows what would have made her heart complete in those moments. If she can find what her heart needs, and if she can then provide it to herself, the wound will no longer need to hold the space within the old information. If the conscious you of today can create that new space, then the wounded part of your heart can have the freedom to let go and shift into the new space of harmony and healing that you have created.

Chloe closed her eyes and pictured the little girl at the dinner table. She could see her short curly hair and the T-shirt that she had been wearing because it was field-trip day at school. She could see the dishes on the table, and she could hear her father's voice. She could feel her heart get heavy as she watched her father disregard her excitement. She rewound the image in her mind, so that she could make the shifts that she needed. She once again focused on the curly-headed girl and her bright orange shirt, but this time it was the conscious version of her today coming to the table. She sat down with a smile on her face ready to fully engage with that adorable little person at the end of the table.

"What is it that my heart needed to hear? What kind of interaction would this little person need to feel connected and heal the wound of separation?" she thought to herself. She took a moment to think about it, and then she began to engage with her.

She watched the little girl turn to her and their eyes met. She could see the excitement light up her face. "Guess what happened today?" the little girl asked.

"Well, that is a big smile you have on your face, Chloe, so something amazing must have happened at school," she said to the girl, as she looked directly at her. "Oh, it was amazing! The whole third grade got to go to the bird sanctuary! You will never believe what happened!" the little girl said, with her eyes wide and bright. "Well let me guess, did a bird talk to you?" the conscious version of her asked. "Yes, but that was not the best part! A bird got loose from one of the cages, and it flew all around us and then landed on me!" she said, so excited she almost fell out of her chair. "That is amazing. You know, it is very good luck to have a bird land on you. It's just like Snow White. All of the animals loved her so much that they would flock to her. You must have something very special inside of you for a bird that just got freed from it cage to come back and land on you."

"I didn't think of it like that. She could have gone anywhere I suppose." "She sure could have, but she chose you to land on and become friends with. That little bird will always be a beautiful story for you, and she will be able to remind you of just how special you are." "You mean, so whenever I see a bird, I can think of her and how she picked me to be friends with?" "Exactly, I have always known how special you are, Chloe, but today even the birds in the sky knew it." With that, the little girl's face lit up even more. She was completely connected to her heart and her story.

The conscious Chloe watched as the younger version of herself finished her dinner in a blissful state. After dinner, she took the little girl by the hand, and lead her to the wingback chair in the study. She pulled her into her lap and they looked at a bird book together. They were able to find the kind of bird that had landed on her during the field trip. Chloe watched the images pass through her mind as if they were washing away the pain that was found in the old information. She hugged the girl tightly and told her how much she loved her and how lucky she was to have her in her life. "No matter what happens in your day, good or bad. I will always be here to listen." She looked into the little girl's smiling face and she told her that she would always be there. She watched the little girl light up even more with those words. They both took in a deep breath and hugged each other again. Chloe could barely recognize the old wound. All she could see from this place was love and connection.

In this part of step four, Chloe was able to lift up the old information around the wound. As she engaged with that wounded part of herself, she was able to begin the healing process. To create the final part of the shift that will allow her to fully create harmony within her heart, Chloe will need to take that inward action one step further. As Chloe engages with new information that comes in around her, she needs to turn inward and interact with the same open-hearted love that she gave to the wounded girl. Chloe taught that part of herself that she can be heard and that she is incredibly loved. Now Chloe can live from this shifted place. From the moment of the shift, and forward, she will be able to engage from the place in her heart that is filled with love and tenderness. She can allow the old information to drift off and the new information to become her truth.

Once she embraces that level of the shift, she can engage outward through the cleared space where the old information once was. Where there was once hesitation to engage because she had been let down, she can now completely engage, knowing that her heart is full and worthy of holding love and connection. She can easily feel the difference between having an empty and guarded heart that holds longing as its only companion, and a full heart that knows love and that is completely connected and engaged. The full heart can be free, just like that bird, and can also find a place of connection, just like that bird, as well.

We have looked at how to use the mirrors and reflections that your heart calls in when there is old information that longs to be shifted. Now let's look at how to use the mirrors and reflections of the positive and full areas of your heart. Your heart holds your whole story and all of its nuances. It is important to remember that the information that you may be calling in can also be a reflection or mirror of beautiful places within that story and your heart. Your information is not always about breaking patterns to help you move closer to a conscious place. It can also be about basking in and appreciating how far you have come. Your information can be about the brilliant and wonderful things that you have created within your story. The mirrors and reflections can be about helping you live into the beautiful parts of your being, rather than letting them get lost in the everyday shuffle. These positive reflections of your heart may be the information that you need to help you understand that you are on the perfect path, or in perfect sync with your life.

Interacting with the positive mirrors and reflections is very similar to interacting with challenging ones. You first have to step up to the mirror and actively look at the situation or information in front of you. Remember that looking and seeing have a subtle but distinct difference. Seeing requires a higher level of action. As you truly see the information, you begin to engage with it. That is what leads you into the second step.

Once you begin to engage with the information, you move directly into step two, where you identify the information that your heart wants you to see.

Remember, you can usually boil down the information into a statement. Once you have the information narrowed down to a statement, it's a little bit easier to claim it.

In step three, you recognize why you have called in the situation as a mirror. It is in this step that you might notice the difference in positive reflections versus mirroring challenges. With the challenging reflections, you may find links to old information, but with the positive ones you find links to the perfection within the new information. You can use the space that you create to bask in the harmony that you are experiencing.

Recognition then leads you to interaction, which is step four. It is important to consciously engage with these positive mirrors. The positive reflections help you see that you are on track toward where your heart wants to go. As you consciously engage with these mirrors and reflections, the truth and brilliance of what they represent will become undeniable to you. This allows them to transform from being just part of your story to becoming positive cellular memories that you can hold on to and use in future situations. They will resonate to the core of your heart. When you are that connected to your heart, you are in perfect harmony with all that is. From this place, every cell in your body will feel lifted and full of light and love. These connected moments can act as indicators or road signs to show you that you are moving in the right direction.

Patrick's Story: Positive Mirrors and Reflections

NOW THAT WE HAVE REVIEWED THE STEPS AGAIN as they link up with the positive information that our hearts call in, we can look at an illustration of how this can manifest. I would like to introduce you to Patrick. He is an artist in his thirties whose story will illustrate what it can look like to identify and engage with positive mirrors and reflections.

Let's first get a little background information on Patrick, so that you can see how the mirror and reflection that we are going to look at fits into place in his story. Patrick grew up in a typical American household. He is one of two children and his parents are still together today. He and his brother grew up in a neighborhood where they had lots of friends to play with on their block. The family dog would run behind the two brothers as they rode their bikes to meet up with their friends. Overall, Patrick had a pleasant childhood. As he meandered through his teenage years and his early twenties, he found himself doing just that, *meandering* through them. There were great adventures as well, along with great love, but there was also great loss and disappointment that caught him off guard. As he moved further through his twenties, he found himself feeling unsettled.

Patrick knew early on that creativity was a strong part of who he was, and who he wanted to become. Before he knew it, he was an artist making and selling his work. Even though he had already proved to himself and others how talented he was, there was always a part of him that questioned his own worth and purpose. This was not the only area that gave him ample information to work with. He also found lots of information in his relationships with women. By nature Patrick was a lover, not a fighter. He enjoyed women and all that they brought to the table. Over the years he had built several strong friendships with women. He had a handful of close girlfriends in his life as well as enjoyable lovers, but even in these relationships he found himself unsettled and constantly questioning.

There was a woman in his life, Anna, who he seemed to be strangely connected to. They had been friends for a few years, and had been lovers off and on through those years. From the first time they met, he found himself easily connecting with her. They would have long talks about life, and he found that being around her, and with her, allowed him to connect to deep parts of his heart. You would think that interaction would be easy, but often what he found was that, although the interaction was easy, the information that would surface through the interaction would be challenging. As he began to engage with his story more, he started to see that she was a safe mirror for his heart to uncover information. He was able to engage with her enough to gather the information, and then disengage enough to find his way through it. Some of the reflections that he found with her as his mirror were rooted in fear and insecurity. They talked around and about where their hearts were. It was almost as if, by checking in with each other, they were checking in with themselves. Over the years he had also seen the reflection of longing and separation. The interaction with her was never unpleasant; challenging at times, but never unpleasant. However, the information that it reflected back to him sometimes could be very uncomfortable. It showed him how wounded his heart still was, and how he was still separated from the things that he wanted in his life.

It had been a year or so since the last time they had interacted with each other. In that time, he had worked on the information that his heart called in. His confidence in his art was getting stronger. He was slowly coming to a place where he trusted that this passion that he had for the things he was creating was a solid enough purpose to live into without questions. He had been in a relationship with a woman who had helped him make great shifts in his understanding of love. While the romantic part of the relationship had come to an end, he had been able to be fully engaged with her. This allowed the love to shift and remain in his life.

This is the point where the illustration begins. Patrick had recently been accepted into an art program in the Northwest. He was going to receive funding to spend two years creating and building his body of work. As part of the program, he would be teaching—something that he truly enjoyed. It was a great opportunity for him, and he was excited to make the change. When he started to make a list of people he wanted to say good-bye to, he found himself adding Anna's name to the list. Even though it had been a long time since they last talked, he couldn't imagine leaving without saying good-bye to her and telling her all about this new adventure he was going to take on. So he called her, and they set up a time to meet.

When she walked up behind him and put her arms around him, it was as if no time had passed since they last met. They sat down and began filling each other in on all of the amazing things that had been happening in their lives. He told her about the move, and the fellowship, and how excited he was about where it seemed to be going. He shared with her how he was able to love again in a relationship, and how wonderful it was to feel that love, even after he and his lover had broken up. She told him about how she was finally writing the book that she had secretly told him she wanted to write almost five years before that moment. She shared with him how she was being drawn farther into embracing love and letting go of the fear. They sat there talking and witnessing each other's lives, and for the first time in their friendship, both lives were full of joy, connection, hope, and fulfillment of dreams. In the past, their friendship brought up reflections of fear that lead to stagnation. They always had fun together, but there was an undercurrent of pain that came with the fear that they both embodied. As they sat there catching up, they could look into the mirror of each other's hearts and see that their fear had been replaced with endless possibility. They were each completely tapped in and connected to the fullness within their hearts and their stories.

As they sat outside, under the moon and the stars, they laughed and completely enjoyed the new space that they were creating. Patrick moved his knees so that they met with Anna's. As they smiled at each other, Anna reached into her pocket and pulled out a tiny envelope. She handed it to him and said, "I wrote this out for you, just in case I didn't have the opportunity to tell you. Because this evening has been so amazing, I know that I can tell you face to face." "What does it say, or what is it that you want to tell me?" he asked, with a smile. "I want you to know how glad I am to have you in my life. I have learned so much about my heart by having you as my friend. I am truly grateful that you are who you are, and that you have created love with me. It doesn't matter how far away you travel, there will always be love for you in my heart." He leaned in and hugged her. His heart felt so full because he felt the same way and knew that it was true for both of them. "I feel the same way about you Anna," he said, as he pulled back to see her face. "Can you believe how far we have come?" he said, with a laugh. "It's kind of amazing, I am very proud of us," she said, feeling very pleased. "I love that we are here," he said, as he gave her a high-five that turned into another hug. "I love that we are here, too. I also love that we are at a place were we can say this to each other. I want you to keep the note so if you ever forget, you will have it in writing," she told him.

They continued to fall deeper into each other's excitement as they shared the details of where they were going. The possibilities were endless, and they spent the rest of the evening marveling in the truth of that, and appreciating the relationship that they had created.

As Patrick drove home, he thought back on the evening. He thought about the different times that his heart had called Anna in as information. They had created a dialogue through so many different phases in their lives. He had seen reflections of his heart and how he was progressing or standing still in his own story just by engaging with her over the years. This time, the information felt dramatically different to him. As he looked back at the evening, he knew that whatever was making it feel so different was important information for him. If he consciously walked through it and paid attention to what his heart was trying to tell him by calling her into his story in this way, it might help him down the road. Not to mention, the information felt so good to him that it was easier to be curious about why it was there.

He stepped up to the information of their interaction from that evening and began to look at it more closely. He thought about the laughter and how familiar and comfortable it was to be around her. There was an ease and pleasure to telling her about his upcoming adventure. She knew how far he had come, and it was as if it deepened the delight she had for him. She had arrived at this great place in her life where all the fear that she had been carrying seemed to be gone, and in its place was a sense of possibility. When she talked about her project and how it allowed her to step into her true purpose, he could feel the certainty in it. They both seemed to have this great momentum that was carrying them forward farther into their purposes. Every sign in the world was showing them that they were exactly where they were supposed to be, and the best part was that any hesitation that might have been there before was now gone.

All of the information that he stepped up to and was looking at was brilliant. It was as if he was standing in a hall of mirrors where all of the information was reflecting something positive back to him. From here, he needed to see which part of it his heart wanted him to claim as his own. He remembered that there was a subtle difference between looking at the information in the mirror and seeing the reflection as it pertained to his heart. He needed to see what it was that his heart was calling in, so that he could identify it and claim it as his own.

As he thought about the evening, he reminded himself that it was less about her. It would be easy to get lost in what it was that they created and leave it at that, but he wanted more than a memory of a wonderful evening; he wanted to find his information in that brilliant mirror. As he looked through the information, the thing he kept coming back to had to do with the fear being gone. It's the biggest difference that he had seen in her, and as he began to look at it, he saw it in himself. The fear had faded into the distance, and the hesitation that manifested because of the fear also seemed to no longer have a place. This was *his* information that his heart had called in. He claimed it has his own. "I no longer need to feel fear about my future, and I no longer need to be hesitant as I engage in it."

As he claimed his information and moved forward to recognize why he had called it in, he began to get even more excited. He had called this information in to create possibility and openness for his story. Without the fear and hesitation, there was endless possibility. In this new fearless space he had created, he could now begin to fully live into that endless possibility. By knowing this and claiming it, Patrick was able to bask in it as truth. He had called in this mirror so that he could see this freeing reflection that allowed him to become the person that he needed to be to live into what it was that he was creating in his life. With the absence of fear and the emergence of endless possibility, he was free to fully engage in his purpose.

This was all information that, on some level, he knew, but by using his interaction with Anna as a mirror, he could engage with it consciously, allowing him to use all of it as his own personal truth. A simple situation in his day transformed into the conscious filling of his heart, and the beauty of that reflection could flood into every cell of his being. From this point forward, Patrick knew this incredible truth about himself and embodied it in every cell of who he is. If he ever begins to feel that hesitation sneaking in, he can stop it by simply leaning into the truth that his heart had mirrored back to him in this situation. The reflection of the situation was so clear to him that he will always be able to call on this truth that he had learned as easily and as clearly as he can recall a memory. From this place of conscious recognition, Patrick can bask in the brilliance of the information that his heart called in and know that it is truly part of his heart and his story.

As you interact with the mirror and reflection process, remember that your heart is at the center of your information. Whether the information in your mirror is challenging you to move through tougher information, or information that is more positive, know that you can use it to help you. The information is yours, and if you can consciously interact with it, you will be closer to finding harmony in the story that is your life.

CHAPTER 5

The Stream–Kayak Principle

HE FIRST FOUR CHAPTERS HAVE SET THE STAGE for chapter five, The Stream–Kayak Principle. Chapter one helped you understand the importance of awakening to your story. Chapter two showed you the value of living completely into your life, and only *your* life. Chapter three taught you how to look at your information differently, and chapter four showed you the importance of using the mirrors and reflections of your heart. As you begin to let go of the old patterns of projecting your information onto other people, you are left with the freedom to move through your own information without being tied to and tangled up in that of other people. From that place of freedom, you can interact with others rather than reacting to them, just as you get to interact with your information rather than reacting to it.

The Stream–Kayak Principle is designed to help you navigate through the information that comes into your everyday life. One of the exceptional aspects of using this principle is that it broadens your consciousness. As your consciousness grows, you will be given the opportunity to make choices about how you interact with the information that comes your way, whatever it may be. When using this principle, you begin to look at the experiences that come into your life as friendly information that is there to help you. Reaction slowly takes a backseat to conscious interaction and negativity moves aside to make room for positive acceptance.

Practicing this principle becomes second nature to you as you experience the benefits it provides. This chapter outlines the structure of the principle and illustrates each facet that its practice encompasses. First, you embody the essence of living downstream. Second, you learn to identify trouble in the water. Third, you navigate through the information that caused the troubled water.

We are going to start by getting you acquainted with the feeling of living downstream. You will learn how to set your conscious attention to find downstream interaction in your everyday life. Then, once you have a sense of the ideal situation, you learn how to use the principle to navigate through trouble in your stream. If you can't embrace life as a downstream process, you are forced to interact with life from a troubled place in the water.

Next, you must learn how to identify these trouble spots in the water. This part of the principle provides you with the vocabulary needed to figure out how you are situated within your story. You may be out of your kayak completely. You may be paddling your boat upstream against the current, or it could be that you have two people in a boat built for one. In each of these situations, you are working against yourself, and are therefore unable to live completely into that brilliant downstream flow of life. This part of the principle will help you identify where you actually are in relation to your kayak, and your consciousness.

Finally, you will move on to the third of the principle's techniques—navigating through the information. Once you are conscious of your situation, you can begin to navigate through the information that brought you there. This is the juiciest part of the process. For every situation you find yourself in, there is information that led you there. With this technique, you will be able to actually put that information to use to create changes and shifts for yourself. The structure that emerges when this principle is in play can help you move beyond the troubled water.

You will be introduced to four people during this chapter who will each illustrate an area of trouble in the water. Olivia's story will illustrate what it's like when two people are in one kayak. Emma will show us what it feels like to identify and navigate through an experience of paddling upstream. Andrew will show you what happens when you are not in your kayak, and Elizabeth will illustrate what it's like to be kicked out of someone else's kayak. Before we engage in their stories, let's first get you engaged in a downstream life.

Step One: Embracing a Life Downstream

LET'S START BY CONSIDERING LIFE AS A STREAM or a river that is naturally flowing downstream. Now let's make it personal to you. This river is your life. Try to picture it. Now, let's say that each person has a kayak that is meant to keep him or her afloat in the stream of life. Each kayak is designed specifically for each individual. As you move along the river, everything you need is right there, part of your kayak. I want you to stop and become consciously aware of all that is encompassed in this statement for a moment. "Everything you need as you move through life is right there for you." Read the sentence a couple more times. *Everything* **you** *need* **as you move through the river is right there, part of the kayak.** As you learn the principle, you will see just how true this is.

Now visualize yourself sitting in your kayak afloat on the river. Create a vivid, almost tangible, image in your mind. Identify the color and shape of your kayak so that you know it's yours. Imagine your fingers running over the smooth outer shell of the boat. Is it built of wood, or fiberglass? Really make it your own. Does it have stripes on it? If so, what colors are they? If you have a good picture of it in your mind, it will be easier for you to integrate the principle into your thought process.

A river, in this case your life, has a downward flowing movement. This downward current is the inherent flow of nature. As each person in his kayak floats on the water, the natural tendency is to follow the current downstream. Picture yourself in your kayak and feel that natural pull flowing downstream. Now, think about the times in your life when there was ease, when you felt like you were in perfect rhythm—in unison with your surroundings. Think about a time when you felt completely in sync with every aspect of your life. This sensation of effortlessness, when you feel no struggle against life, is the downstream movement. You are in the flow of the river of life and nestled safely and harmoniously in your boat. This is the ideal circumstance, life moving downstream in perfect harmony.

Let's get you more acquainted with how you relate to your kayak by looking at times when you were in it and moving downstream. Think back, and dig a little, I want you to find something that resonates with you on a cellular level. A cellular memory is a memory that when recalled, triggers a cellular response. A positive cellular memory is one that when recalled, brings a smile to your face, laughter in your belly, goose bumps to your skin, or a welling of happiness to your heart. Holding on to positive cellular memories can be very helpful and in many situations can be used as a tool to keep you in your kayak. Let's find a memory where you can feel that downstream flow in every cell of your being. Don't worry if this is hard at first. Just be tender with yourself. If it's a challenge, you can make a point to consciously be on the lookout for that downstream feeling in the future. Once you are conscious of what downstream situations are like, you will begin to see them and highlight them in your everyday life. Keep in mind that "downstream" may look a little different for each of us.

Another good way to see yourself in your kayak, in flow with the river of life, is by using positive cues or trigger words. Each of us is living our very own story. Within that story there are words that act as cues that trigger connection to your heart. They are words that link you to memories or ideas that trigger a positive response from your mind and heart. Some examples are: love, ocean, stillness, travel, strength, peace, adventure, laughter, music, or play. More often than not, when you're connected to your heart, you will find yourself sitting happily in your kayak floating downstream. Positive cellular memories are memories that you have of a time when you were connected to your heart. Cue or trigger words can help you get in touch with these memories. This will help you build up your cellular memory bank. For now, while learning and building on the first step of the Stream–Kayak Principle and embracing life downstream, let's practice with the word *rhythm*. Let's see how the word *rhythm* can trigger a positive cellular memory to get you in your kayak with the sensation of downstream movement.

There are many ways to use the word *rhythm* in a person's everyday life. Think back and see if you can remember a time where you were in rhythm with your surroundings. Most people travel from place to place within their day. Let's start there. Driving is an experience that can easily be associated with being in rhythm. Let's paint a picture that you might have experienced: You were driving down the road and every streetlight turned green as you approached it, or perhaps you moved through traffic without having to hit your brakes. It was as if you were in perfect cadence with every car and light on the road. Let's say you moved with ease around cars as if the path was laid out specifically for you. Maybe you arrived at your destination and a parking spot right up front was waiting for you, as if it were reserved just for you. Things fall into place. Like gears of a clock, you are effortlessly in perfect rhythm. Maybe you got into your car and your favorite song started to play on the radio. For those who don't drive, maybe you found yourself running errands and you walked up to the bus or train stop and waited only a moment before it arrived. You hopped on and there was a seat waiting for you. Each store you walked into had exactly what you were looking for, and, lo and behold, one of the things was on sale. This is you floating downstream in your kayak. You are in rhythm; your kayak is effortlessly gliding through the water, and you are basking in the sun.

Maybe the cellular memory that is triggered by the word *rhythm* is pictured in a whole day. You woke up on a Sunday, and went out for your weekly farmers' market stop. You were with people that you love, and you were enjoying the day. You went to visit some friends who were moving out of the country, and you found out that they were actually only moving a couple of hours away. Then you happened to run into another friend that you hadn't seen in a while, and you both just happened to be free, so you got to spend the afternoon together. Around every corner there was a surprise that lifted the heart, and if you had been a moment off, you might have missed the whole thing. You were in perfect rhythm with your day.

As you use the word *rhythm* to trigger cellular memories, your mind and heart might take you to the ocean. Maybe there was a time when you walked up to the ocean, and you felt the essence of your being in perfect harmony with everything around you. You think back on that time, and you smell the salt in the air. It was all so inviting, and being in that moment was effortless. Your feet hit the warm sand, and you felt as if you were home. The cool air off the water called your name as you made your way to where the sand and the water meet. They pooled around you, as if in excitement for your existence. You took a deep breath, and with that breath you felt your heart swell. You could not be in a more perfect place for that moment. The rhythm of the waves that crashed at your ankles almost followed the pace of your breath. Standing there, where the water meets the earth, you felt as if you were part of something bigger. You were a small part of that vast ocean and those millions of grains of sand. You were part of their perfect rhythmic story, just as they were part of yours. Recalling a positive cellular memory like this would bring you right to your heart, and there you are in your kayak headed downstream.

Let's look at one more possible way that the word *rhythm* could trigger a positive cellular memory. If you play an instrument, or if you are a music enthusiast, the positive cellular memory triggered by the word *rhythm* may be wrapped up in music. It could be the memory of a piece of music. When you hear the notes played, it is as if your heart meets each chord and every cell in your body follows along to its rhythm. You close your eyes to take it in even further, and you are transported to a place where all the noise of life melts away. You are not only being carried by the rhythm of the music but by the rhythm of the downstream movement. Maybe you have a memory of when you picked up your instrument, and as you played, you felt in perfect rhythm. Your lips hit the mouthpiece, or your fingers touched the strings, and you began to feel body, mind, and heart acting in perfect rhythm as you created your music. It was as if every cell of your being reacted to that rhythm and the vibrations that you created. You were there, brilliantly connected to your heart, and now the memory floats in every cell of your being. As you recall it, you are again connected to your heart. In that connection you are in your kayak moving gracefully in perfect downstream rhythm.

In the Stream–Kayak Principle, downstream in your kayak is the ideal place to be. The goal is to be effortlessly floating downstream in your kayak, and being connected to your heart is the most effective way to do this. Whether you are trying to get back to a positive place or are just starting to find out what downstream feels like, use your positive cellular memories to find your kayak and the current heading downstream. Now that you have generally identified what downstream can look and feel like, keep those downstream thoughts in the forefront of your mind. Try to keep your eyes and heart open to how you move downstream in your everyday life. The positive cellular memories are designed to help you get pointed downstream in your kayak, so build them up whenever you can. You may find that when you start to look for downstream situations, they are all around you. When you encounter them, make a mental note. Acknowledge and appreciate them as you sit in your kayak and flow brilliantly downstream.

Step Two: Identifying the Trouble in the Water

NOW THAT YOU HAVE AN UNDERSTANDING of what floating downstream can feel like, you can move on to the next step. Step two is identifying trouble in the water. Let's identify situations that may create trouble in your water. If you can identify these tricky situations and you have a principle to help navigate through the information in those situations, then you can get your kayak back on the downstream track. If you identify the trouble in the water, employ the principle and "be gentle with yourself" as you come into awareness of it. There are few people who have lived a life without some sort of trouble in their water. Everything in your life is information that can bring you to a more conscious and happy place, if you use it. Troubled water is no different. To get to step three, navigating through the information, you must first be aware of the information so that you can use it. By identifying the trouble, you take the first step toward shifting it. Sometimes, you won't see why things are not working or even realize that things are not working in your life until something big happens to wake you up. Sometimes, the trouble feels like little annoying hiccups, small information that keeps coming up. Other times, it feels like the information is so big that it's hard to get a handle on it. Using the Stream–Kayak Principle, you can become more conscious of what is working and what is not so you can navigate more quickly and effectively toward what does work. Identifying the trouble in your water is the next step toward living downstream.

In the "identifying trouble in the water" portion of the Stream–Kayak Principle there are three main scenarios to look for that create trouble in the water: putting two people in a one-person kayak, paddling upstream, and being out of your kayak altogether. We are going to walk through each one of these scenarios using some examples. As you look at the examples in this section, they may or may not resonate with you. The goal is for you to get the hang of the principle. If the examples bring up too much information, take your time. Keep in mind that you may just need the information in the chapters ahead in order to navigate back to a calm and downstream flow. On the other hand, even if you find that none of the examples resonate with you, by the end of the section you will have an understanding of the principle, and you can apply it to your unique story and life. The examples provided illustrate the principle so that you can use it better and can start identifying places where you have juicy information to navigate through. Before we dig into the examples, let's look at step three.

Step Three: Navigating Through the Information

THIS IS THE STEP IN WHICH YOU NAVIGATE through the information. It is the natural downstream progression from step two. To navigate through the information, you must examine it in phases. In phase A, you identify the statement that helped you create the trouble in the water. In phase B, you look for contrast in your situation. This is where you stay with your trouble in the water, versus floating downstream. Once you have created contrast, you are able to move into phase C, where you consciously shift your statement so that you can reposition your kayak to its naturally downstream-facing direction. This creates room and sets the intention for how you interact in phases D and E. In phases D and E, you go deeper into your heart and make conscious shifts in your story. Phase D is where you gather information about how you came to have difficulty in the water that is your life. In phase E, you embrace the information you have gathered, so you can harmonize your heart. *Identify* your statement; *Acknowledge* the contrast; *Shift* your statement; *Gather* your information; *Embrace* and *Harmonize* your heart and story.

Pay attention to the structure of the principle as we explore the examples. Until the principle becomes second nature, you can use this outline to help you find where you are in the process, either in the illustration, or in your own story.

Step 1: **Embracing Life Downstream**

Step 2: **Identifying Trouble in the Water**
Two People, One Kayak
Paddling Upstream
Out of Your Kayak

Step 3: **Navigating Through the Information**
Phase A: Identifying Your Statement
Phase B: Creating and Acknowledging Contrast
Phase C: Shifting Your Statement Consciously

Phase D: Gathering Information
- *Identify the essence behind your identified statement*
- *Identify the first time in your life when you experienced that essence*
- *Find the root of the information*
- *Identify the old pile of information where it initiated*

Phase E: Embracing Information to Harmonize Your Heart
- *Go back to the first time you felt that essence and shift your statement there*

Now that you have the structure and information behind the structure, you can begin to investigate and understand the examples of how the principle can be put into practice.

Example One: Trouble in the Water
Putting Two People in a One-Person Kayak

IN YOUR KAYAK, THERE IS ONLY ONE SEAT. Each person gets one kayak. If you find yourself in someone else's kayak, or if you are inviting or pulling someone else into your kayak, then there is going to be trouble in the water. Your kayak was not made to accommodate more than one person and will not hold up in the stream. Doubling up in a one-person vessel is something that happens a lot. We buy into the idea that we may be safer with someone else in our kayak with us. We may be taken care of if we share a kayak. This is not so. If you are relying on someone else for your consciousness or happiness, then at some point in the journey there will be significant trouble in your waters. This situation is created in relationships with parents, siblings, friends, and even coworkers. You may also see this in a relationship with lovers, partners, and spouses.

Look at some of the "two people in a one-person kayak" inner dialogue. As you do, you should keep a couple of things in mind: Sometimes the hardest thing is to be honest with yourself. Remember that anything that comes up is just information. Take self-judgment out of the equation. As you become more conscious and honest with your information, remember to be tender with yourself. You are just beginning to learn.

Now, try to see if any of these examples sound familiar or resonate with aspects of your dialogue with the people in your life.

- ৡ Love me, so I can feel love.
- ৡ I don't want to be by myself; be with me, so I don't feel alone.
- ৡ Be with me, so I will feel complete, because you complete me.
- ৡ "I am tired of being depressed and sad; be with me, so I can feel happiness.
- ৡ Date me and marry me, so I can prove to myself that I am worthy.
- ৡ Protect me, so I can feel safe.
- ৡ "Sit with me in this pain or pleasure of life, so my feelings can be witnessed.
- ৡ See me, so I can have an identity.
- ৡ Hear me and what I am saying, so my opinions can be validated.
- ৡ Create this partnership with me, so you can provide me with all that I lack in my life.

Anytime you say, "Do this, so I can . . ." you have placed two people in a one-person kayak and trouble is not far off. Your kayak will eventually sink with two people in it. Before it sinks, the other person may decide to push you out of his or her kayak, leaving you stranded in the water. When there are two people in one kayak, your downstream movement cannot *flow*. You may be moving downstream, but it will feel sluggish or stagnant—not flowing. Two people can survive in one kayak, but do you want to merely survive, or do you want to live fully with a free heart?

Now, begin to navigate through the information according to the phases in step three. Start by moving through the phases specific to this example. In phase A, you will identify the other person in the kayak and the statement that put both of you in one kayak. Next, in phase B, you will look for the contrast between being crammed in a kayak with someone else and floating on your own. When the contrast is created, you can then move on to phase C, where you will consciously shift the statement that put more than one person in your kayak. Once you change the statement, you can each position yourself in your own kayak. When you have the new positioning, you will have the freedom to gather the information you need in order to move to phase D. In that phase, you will navigate to a place where you can embrace the information and harmonize your heart back to a position where you are in your own kayak and headed downstream.

Look at the "two people in a one-person kayak" inner dialogue again, and see how you can move through this method in phases to give you the freedom to brilliantly flow downstream in your own kayak.

Let's look at phase A where you identify the person and the statement that put two people in one boat. The person interacting with you in this statement could be anyone. For this example, let's identify them as your lover or partner. Now, let's identify your statement as, "Love me, so I can feel love." If this statement does not resonate with you, just read along, paying attention to the principle. Once you get the hang of the phases, you will be able to plug in any statement that may pertain to you directly. "Love me, so I can feel love." Sounds good at first, right? The statement is actually a bit tricky because, when you create love with someone, more often than not, you feel the other person's love. However, by saying "Love me, so I can feel love," you are tethering your conscious awareness of yourself and your love to the other person. This makes you and your happiness dependEnt on someone else. This is a lot of pressure to put on another person, and it's a job that no one can keep up with. Having two people in one kayak is just not sustainable.

In phase B, you create contrast. Let's create some contrast so that you can more easily see the difference between floating downstream in your own kayak and barely staying afloat with two people in one kayak. In this case, the contrast is illustrated by comparing dependEnt lifeline love (two people, one kayak) with a free-flowing gifted love (two people, two kayaks). DependEnt love says, "Something in me is broken, and I must have your love to mend this broken spot in my heart." Gifted love says, "My heart is whole, and I would like to give you this love that I experience when you are in my life." Lifeline love says, "Create love with me because my heart is not enough on its own, and if I have your love, too, I can fill those empty spaces." Free flowing love says, "Let's create love together, so we can make something bigger than the two of us, and see what we build from there." In one situation, love is working hard to fill and support the heart. All the energy is focused on the work that has to be done. You are tethered to each other, working hard to keep one overloaded kayak above water. In the other situation, love is creating, building, and experiencing for the heart. The energy is upward and outward as you freely move along with everything you are creating. Your heart is focused and you are moving forward downstream.

When you are tethered to each other by being in one kayak, you end up knocking into each other. You may have started out sweetly nestled on each other's laps, but then someone's leg falls asleep and you try to move to a position that is more comfortable, but it's not easy. One of you may get an elbow in the eye, or a foot in the ribs. There is just not enough room in the kayak for each of you to move about comfortably. You find part of the love that was once so blissfully filling your heart turning into resentment. The emotional wound of the foot in the ribs just doesn't seem to heal, or you just can't let it go. You may say to the other person in the kayak, "You're not loving me right, or enough, because I can still feel gaps in my heart." Things may be okay, but you can't seem to achieve that downstream flow because your kayak is just too weighted down.

By creating contrast, you can start to see the difference between being in your own kayak and squeezing into someone else's. From there, you can start moving yourself back into your own kayak. In this example, you are using a partner or lover, but remember, in your own life you might be caught in anyone else's kayak, or you may be jumping from kayak to kayak. The statement, "Love me, so that I can feel love," may have you caught in your parent, sister, brother, or even your child's kayak.

Before you approach the next phase, I would like you to recognize that, if you are sharing a kayak now, your interaction with the other person in the kayak is providing you with a brilliant way to tap into your story and your heart. After all, being in someone else's kayak is just information, and if you can get back in your own kayak, there is a good chance you will soon be floating your way downstream again. You will have learned, and evolved, and tapped into a deeper place in your heart, bringing you freedom and joy. Appreciation is an important thing to keep in mind as you apply this principle to your everyday life.

While you move through the phases, you are navigating through your story. In our illustration you saw a person and statement that created trouble in the water and you examined the contrast in the statement. Now, you can move toward changing the statement and repositioning the kayaks, gathering the information and embracing the information to harmonize the heart and get back into your own kayak so you can move forward downstream.

In phase C, you learn how to change the instigating statement. When you change your statement, you set an intention for yourself to make the changes you need to float downstream. Big changes are possible when you set an intention for yourself. It is important to create a statement that gives you room to interact freely with your heart. When working through the trouble of having two people in one kayak, you must create a statement that will cut the strings that keep you tethered together in that single kayak. The instigating statement was, "Love me, so I can feel love." DependEnt, lifeline-like love is the tethering string, so you know this is the place to start. Now, change the statement of dependEnt love to one that provides free-flowing, gifted love. To do this, you must create a statement where you stand independently filled with love. For example, "My heart is filled with love." With the tethering concept removed, you can now add to the statement to allow for another kayak, so that you each have your own. "I recognize this love I have in me, in you." When you put the two parts together the statement becomes, *My heart is filled with love, and I know it so well that I can recognize the same love in you.* The statement feels strong, and it leaves room for both parties to bask in the love. Now let's put the two statements side by side, so you can see the contrast. "Love me, so I can feel love," versus "My heart is filled with love, and I know it so well that I can recognize the same love in you." The first statement is demanding and limiting, while the second is giving and open. You have created a wonderful contrast and a brilliantly refined guiding statement. This change in statement has clearly set your intention for the shift from one kayak to two.

With the new statement comes new kayak poisoning. Let's look at the new position of your kayak. *My heart is filled with love, and I know it so well that I can recognize the same love in you.* "My heart is filled with love," indicates that, now, you are in your kayak, whole and not dependEnt on another human being. "I know it so well that I can recognize it in you," demonstrates that the other person resides in their own kayak apart from you. In this statement, you are both able to move about freely. You get to be you, and the other has an identity apart from you. Both people get to experience love on a deeper and freer level. Deeper because for the first time, every nook and cranny of your heart is filled with the love that you uncovered within yourself without a dependence on the other. Freer, because it is now a gift you exchange, rather than a demand that must be met. Both of you are navigating as whole people, creating and building on the love you each already have in your hearts and beings. In this kayak position, love is a gift you get to share and not an IV being administered to keep your happiness and heart alive.

We have the positioning now—one person in one kayak. In phase D, you gather the information that will take you farther into the heart of your story. Many people stop at the end of phase C. They think it is enough to feel the small amount of freedom that comes when the statement is changed. Their mind is engaged in their story and they feel that connection is enough. The truth is that the guiding statement is just the beginning. Phase D moves the statement from your head into your heart. The heart is where your story is, and where freedom is found. If you can shift your statement in your mind, you are doing well, but if you can shift your statement in your heart, you have made it back into your kayak where there is endless freedom for your heart.

In gathering the information, you come to a conscious understanding of why you were in another person's kayak. You gather the information you need to make your "new statement" a personal truth for yourself. In addition, the information brings to light the intrinsic motivation behind your initial statement. From there, you can explore the first time you felt the underlying essence in your story. After you have the information in your grasp, you learn to embrace the information and find harmony within your heart. Then, you can integrate the healing into your life, allowing you to get back in your own kayak and head downstream.

Olivia's Story: Two People in One Kayak

THE STRUCTURE FOR THE GATHERING AND EMBRACING PART of the principle is easy enough to define, but the information that is gathered and embraced is as unique as each story is unique. Because of the nature of this part of the principle, you need to look at an individual example of this principle in practice. Meet Olivia. She is a beautiful woman in her early thirties. The statement "Love me, so I can feel love" was one that she identified as causing trouble in her water. Let's use the information that she gathered, along with how she navigated her way back to her kayak, to illustrate the steps in this part of the principle.

What does gathering the information look like? First let's explore the underlying essence behind the statement "Love me, so I can feel love," as it happened for Olivia. When Olivia looked at the information, she discovered that, deep inside, she felt an absence of love. She got aboard the other person's kayak in search of the missing love or a replacement for it. She was not even conscious that love was missing at first. All she felt was an unconscious pull toward something that was defining parts of her life and relationships. She knew things didn't seem to work out when she was in love with someone, but she could never figure out why. She spent time blaming the other person and questioning her worth because of this unconscious pull to fill the void. By working through the principle, Olivia discovered that she was asking for another person to fill a void that belonged to her, and it became clear that it was unproductive.

The next part of gathering the information is locating the first time you remember that this underlying sense was a part of your story. When Olivia looked back, she found that she had been asking her past boyfriends and lovers to fill that missing sense of love. She recognized the feeling of chaos that occurs when two people attempt to share one kayak. She understood the struggle to make things work that had pervaded her past relationships. She also found that she gathered pets to create a sense of love around her. She was trying to surround herself with that missing love. All the information she was uncovering was enlightening. Be careful at this point in the process. Sometimes when you turn on a light, you end up seeing much more than you expected. Remember that you are trying to find the *first* time that you encountered that underlying feeling. Take care not to get stuck digging through the old information. The goal is to return to the downstream flow, not to become lost in the trouble in the water. Olivia knew she had been searching for a missing love, so there must have been a time when she thought she lost it. When she focused her energy on looking for the time she lost love, rather than all the times she was trying to find it in other kayaks, she came up with some different information. Olivia found the information in memories of her life as a young girl. The missing love that her heart was trying to fill was the love of her father.

After catching a glimpse of this memory, she quickly retreated from it saying that she knew her father loved her, so that could not be the love that was missing. She experienced a sharp sense of guilt for questioning her father's love. When you look back and gather your information, remember that it is just information. We put lots of attachments on our information. We have scenarios running through our heads with outcomes that flash before our eyes. Acknowledge the reaction to your information. Be tender and honest with yourself and keep the information in its simplest form. Let go of the scenarios and attachments. For Olivia, the simplest form of the information was recognizing that her younger self was missing something. When she was able to let go of her reaction and the imagined outcomes or scenarios wrapped around it, she could let it just be information. The information was that she was missing love and connection that she felt her father could have provided. Once her information had been gathered, she could use it to navigate to a place where her heart was full and she was in her kayak headed downstream.

Let's look now at how to embrace your information so you can harmonize your heart. You can begin embracing the information by reacquainting yourself with your goal, making your new statement truth. Once you have that goal firmly in sight, the conscious you of today can go back and visit the place where the information started and tap into the *you* of that time. Allow yourself to be present in your memory, and listen to the dialogue that comes up. Fully engage in all aspects of the moment through meditation or conscious visualization. Remember to keep the focus on you and your information. From there you can make contact. The *conscious you* of today can go to the *younger you* in that initial place where the information started and help heal the wound that was created back then.

As you navigate through your information and embrace it to harmonize your heart, you must remain focused on the goal you have defined in a guiding statement like, *My heart is filled with love, and I know it so well that I can recognize the same love in you*—your new truth. You started with two people in one kayak, and the goal is to get both of you into your own individual kayaks. This is the goal you are navigating toward. Let's look at what happened when Olivia gathered and embraced her information and navigated back into her own kayak. Olivia's goal is made up of two parts: The first engages the beginning of her new statement, "My heart is filled with love, and I know it so well." Making this part of the statement truth will put her happily in her kayak with her heart full. The second part states, "I can recognize the same love in you." This part of her goal will allow her to engage with her lover/partner in a way that she never has before. She will be able to interact with freedom that moves her inexorably downstream. She can recognize the love that fills her own heart as it is mirrored in the person who is floating beside her. She can share love brilliantly with her partner from a place of openness and independence.

If you remain focused on your goal, then you can navigate through your information. You can consciously return to the past where the initial statement or information began. Olivia went back to interact with her younger self to discover what event had caused her to feel as if she had lost love. She remembered her home as being full of fun and laughter. It was a place where she felt that she had all she needed. Love was abundant and downstream movement came easily. When she took the memory deeper than these initial impressions, she recalled her father having to leave often. She remembered that he had never seemed to stay home very long. His business always took precedence over her and their family. Olivia loved him so much, and she missed him terribly when he was gone. Even though she was very young, she understood that his work was important. Still, she could not stop the feeling of longing for him to be part of all that she was experiencing as a little girl—to be there for her. Every time he had to leave for business it felt like he was saying to her that she didn't matter. She felt like he was saying, "I love this work that I do more than I love you." She began to wonder if he was thinking about work even when he was with her. She found her young self saying, "See me, love me, and stay with me." The younger Olivia's heart was wounded by her perception of this interaction with her father.

The conscious Olivia of today can rationalize the fact that her father had to travel for his work, so the source of her statement was obscured. The key for Olivia was to see that the information was less about her father and more about her. After all, this is not her father's story; it's Olivia's. Olivia can't possibly know her father's mind and heart. She is, in fact, only now uncovering the inner workings of her own story. Rationalizing her father's motivations or worrying about his perception at that time are counterproductive to reaching her goal. She cannot go back in time and make him give her what she was missing. Instead Olivia needed to go back and help herself as a child understand and heal from the wound that was created. This applies to anyone navigating through past information. You must remind yourself that the information is less about the other person and more about you. You cannot change anyone but yourself. Remember asking someone to "Do this so that I can be or feel this other way," only puts you in their kayak. You have all that you need in your kayak. The information that comes to you is yours and is placed in your kayak to help you grow, and evolve, and find a sense of peace and happiness as you move downstream. Navigating your way through it is how you get there. Once Olivia understood that the loss she felt was less about her father and more about her, she could move to a place where she could help her younger self heal the wound that was created. Her focus could be on the younger Olivia and not on her father. This had to happen before the healing could begin.

Remember what the first part of Olivia's goal was: *My heart is filled with love, and I know it.* Your goal statement should be focused and clearly in your mind as you make contact with your younger self who holds the wound created in your past. When you move toward making contact, try not to be attached to the accuracy of the memory and avoid being reactive to what you see. The events will not happen again in exactly the same way they did in your actual past because you will be blending your memories with images that you create to help you heal that place where you found the wound. The conscious you of today is going to go back and initiate a healthy dialogue with your younger self holding the wound. That younger you has been holding this wound for a while, so, as you create a new and healthy dialogue about the wound, you may find that it heals and there is little, if anything, for your younger self to hold on to. Bringing freedom to the younger you will inevitably bring freedom to the present conscious you. The brilliant part of creating the dialogue is that the conscious you of today is the only person in the whole world who can know exactly what to say to the wounded part of yourself to make it better. You have the key to the inner workings of your heart, and you know what might have been missing, or what happened to make that part of you feel wounded. All you need to do is look and listen with your conscious heart. Everything that you need to move through and beyond the wounding is sitting in your kayak with you.

Olivia could see that her wound was the perceived lack of love from her father that she experienced at a young age. She needed to find a way to make her statement truth, and to do that she had to fill her heart with love and know it well enough that she could see it in someone else. To fulfill that part of the goal, she had to make contact with her younger self who was engaging with her father when the wound occurred.

Make contact and go back to the place where the information started, and then take a good look at the *you* of that time. Take some time to see what you were wearing, what your hair looked like; hear your vocal inflections. Be aware of the body language that your younger self used. Appreciate how cute, smart, funny, or precocious you were. Notice how clean or dirty you were, smell the kid sweat or sweetness that you carried then. Look for the innocence and tenderness that were innately yours in youth. Identify with that part of you. Move in closer and bring that image into a setting. Observe your surroundings. Are you in a room or outside? What do you smell and taste? Can you identify any sensations on your skin? Develop the visual details to make this image as visceral as possible. The more you identify with your surroundings and with the image of the younger you, the easier it will be to communicate honestly and meaningfully with your inner child. After you have immersed yourself in that place with your child self, you can move toward making contact. Visualize the conscious you of today approaching the younger you who holds the wound. What is the younger you looking for? What does your wounded self need? Let yourself empathize with what the child is experiencing, take in an awareness of that space, and, as the adult, give your child self what he or she desperately needs.

Bring the conscious you into the picture. Picture the *you* of today entering the space and approaching your child self holding the wound. Tenderly make physical contact with that younger you. Place a hand on the child's knee or head. Get down to eye level and look into the child's eyes. You may find that your child self needs the physical interaction, so invite the younger you into your lap or your embrace. Once you have made physical contact, you can move on to making verbal contact. What is it that this young wounded person needs? You already know, so look into your own younger eyes and tell yourself what your heart needs to hear to help the wound start to heal. You can ask about the wound you are holding and let your younger self explain how and why you are holding it. Interact with the child you in a healthy, loving, and nurturing way to provide healing for the wound. As you move through the conversation, imagine the child letting the wound go until it is no longer something that must be carried. Show your child self that your love and nurturing are constants and that you will always be there, always supporting. Remind the child that you are conscious and listening to your heart now and that means you will always be listening to your child self as well. As you identify with this part of yourself, you can create a dialogue that you can reopen any time throughout any day. This initial contact and exercise is like a guided meditation and might take a little time, space, and more than one attempt. Once you have made your initial contact, if you begin to feel yourself inching your way back into someone else's kayak, ask that younger part of you why. The younger you is the voice for the wounds of your heart. Once the dialogue is started, then you have a very tangible way of determining the root of your struggles and the balm that will heal your wounds.

Let's look at Olivia's story to see how this manifested for her. Keep in mind that no two stories are alike. When Olivia looked closely at her child-self, she appreciated just how precious she was. Her big eyes looked sad, but her face was small and bright. Her hair was light and it had little ringlets at the ends. She was wearing jean shorts and a pretty pink shirt. She found herself in a room, sitting on a chair with the lights out. She could not see much in the room, but there was a little table next to her. Her head was down and she was not talking or moving around. Olivia noticed that her little socks were folded down just perfectly. She was so cute, like a little doll sitting in a dark room.

Now that she had a good picture of the little girl, she was ready to make contact. With her eyes closed, she took a deep breath and pictured herself walking into the room. The younger version of herself didn't even move. Olivia walked over to the little table and turned the lamp on to bring some light into the room. The soft light gave the room a warm glow. Olivia squatted down beside the chair. The little girl's head slowly rose up. Olivia put her hand on the child's little knee. The girl immediately made eye contact. Her big round eyes looked deeply into Olivia's. Olivia smiled at the girl, but the girl did not smile back. She seemed so tired and sad. Olivia realized that the wound she was holding was too heavy for such a little girl, and she must be tired from carrying it. Olivia began to talk to the little girl.

"Hello," she said. The sound of Olivia's voice brought the corners of the little girl's mouth up in a tentative smile.

"Hi," she whispered back.

"Why are you whispering?" Olivia asked.

"I don't want to bother anyone," the precious little girl replied.

"It's okay. You don't need to whisper. I came here just to talk to you, and you can't possibly bother me if I am here to see you," she said lovingly.

The little girl sat up a little straighter on her little chair. "You are here to see me?" The little girl seemed curious.

"Yes, I am. Is that okay with you?" the grown-up Olivia asked. The little girl smiled.

"Sure," the little girl replied.

"Why are you sitting in this dark room all by yourself?" Olivia asked. The girl put her little hand on top of Olivia's and began to play with her fingers. She seemed a little uncomfortable. Her gaze was down, watching her hand in Olivia's when she answered.

"Well, this is my room, and I am waiting for my dad to come home."

"So you're sitting here waiting for him?" Olivia began to understand the image.

She looked up at the grown-up Olivia. "A lot of times my daddy has to leave when we have plans to do something, or even in the middle of us doing something. He helps people, and it is important to help people," she said, as though she had rehearsed the reply.

"Is that what your dad told you?" Olivia asked.

"My daddy and my mommy say that," she replied.

"But it must be hard for you when he leaves," Olivia said, feeling her out.

"I must not be as important as those other people. Or, at least not as important to my daddy," she stated in a very matter-of-fact, yet sad, tone.

"Oh," Olivia said. "Why were all of the lights out in your room?" Olivia asked.

"Right now I am sad, and the color of sad is black and dark, so I turned the light off because I am all alone and sad right now," she said, as her head hung down again.

"Wow," Olivia said, "you sure are smart for knowing what the color of sadness is." This made the little girl smile.

"Where is you dad right now?" she asked.

"Oh, he had to go to work to help more people, I guess. We were going to go to the park. I got all dressed in my park clothes, but we couldn't go, so I went to my room instead. I really didn't want to be by myself today. I wanted to have fun with my daddy," she said as her little chin quivered. "We always have so much fun when we get to play together," she added with a sniffle.

Olivia could feel the sadness welling up in her chest as she sat there with her eyes closed watching the scene play out in her mind. She took a deep breath again. Olivia knew she would need to ask the bigger questions if she was going to find the key to what the child desperately needed. Olivia took the little girl's hands in hers.

"How do you feel about your daddy?" she asked.

"I miss him, and I am mad at him, and mostly I just love him," the child said with another sniffle.

Olivia asked another question. "Do you think he loves you?"

The little girl thought about it for a minute, then answered.

"When I am with him and he makes me laugh, and I sit in his lap, and he reads to me, it makes me happy and I feel lots of love."

"And when he leaves, then what do you feel?" Olivia prodded.

The little girl tucked her head down and said, "I feel like the love goes away." A tear ran down the little girl's cheek.

"He leaves so much that I think he forgets about me. I chased after him one time, but he didn't even turn around. I was crying for him, but getting to work was much more important than me. I don't feel any love when that happens. I always feel like the love can be taken away at any moment, just like my daddy," she said.

By this time, Olivia could feel the child's tears welling up in her own eyes. The conscious Olivia's heart was hurting, as well. The wound was no longer just sitting with the little girl, it was now open for the conscious her, too. Olivia's goal was to know love so well that she could see it in someone else. She could see the love in her younger self. She could see the love, and feel the love within the child. Because this little person was Olivia, she knew exactly what she needed to heal. She needed the love that conscious Olivia of today could easily provide.

Olivia stood up and picked the little girl up in her arms. The little girl clung to her. Her little legs wrapped around Olivia's waist and her arms encircled her neck. Olivia sat in the chair with the little girl still attached to her. Her arms held the little girl just as tightly. She knew that the girl needed to feel the security of that embrace. They sat in the comfort of that security for a long time. Then Olivia knew exactly what she needed to say next:

"Guess what?" Olivia whispered into the child's ear. The girl's answer was all muffled because her head was buried in Olivia's neck. Olivia asked the little girl to look at her. She tenderly brushed the hair out of her eyes and said with a smile, "Guess what?"

"What?" the little girl asked, with her big hopeful eyes looking up at Olivia.

"You will never have to be alone again." The smile on Olivia's face grew bigger as she said it. The little girl looked excited for a moment, then the look changed to confusion.

"How come?" she asked, with her brow furrowed. "How come I won't be alone?"

"Because," Olivia said, as she hugged the girl again. "I will always be here with you."

She paused to let it sink in. Then she went on, "I want to tell you something else, and I want you to listen very closely. Are your good listening ears on?" Olivia asked.

"Oh, yes!" the girl replied, with a smile.

Olivia looked into her big eyes and said, "I love you very much, and you will never have to run after me. I will be here filled with love, so you will never run out of it. I will always be here with you." As she said those words to that hopeful little girl, the tears began to well up again. These were not tears of sadness; this time they were tears of release. Olivia began to feel a tingling around her heart. The ache was shifting, and she could physically feel the healing happening. As she said the words, the little girl was no longer sunken down in the chair and taken over by the darkness of the lonely room. The girl was being loved in the light, and in a nurturing lap with loving arms wrapped around her. As that wound healed for the little girl, it also healed for Olivia.

The little girl put her hands on Olivia's cheeks and said, "I am so glad that you found me. I was trying to be so quiet, but you heard me." The little girl wrapped her arms around Olivia's neck and whispered in her ear.

"I will love you forever, too." Olivia's heart welled up with those words. She sat in that moment of love, fully embracing it. As the love touched every cell of her being, she had another thought.

"I want to tell you something else," Olivia said. "It's about your dad."

"What about my daddy?" the little girl asked.

"It's about you and your daddy's love," Olivia said, as she looked into the girl's big eyes.

"You feel lots of love with your dad when he is with you, right? You told me that you know he loves you when he is reading to you and you are playing and laughing."

"Yes, I do," she said.

"And you said that most of all you love him. That is what you said, right?" Olivia asked, making sure.

"Yes, I do love him very much," the girl said.

"Okay, now that you know you will never be alone again, now that you know I will always be here for you, do you think you can let your daddy be the person who helps people *and* loves you, too? Because we can play, and laugh, and love each other whenever you want, your daddy can just be who he is without you feeling so much sadness."

"Well, that sounds okay, but shouldn't daddies always love their little girls?" she asked, with her brow furrowed again.

"Of course they should, but you cannot see everything that goes on in your daddy's heart. You can't know your daddy's entire story. I bet that he does love you all of the time. I bet that, even when he is gone helping other people, the love he has for you is still alive in his heart. So you see, you can count on love any time of any day. You may be able to see it and feel it with your dad when he's here, and with me when he's not. Plus, you can know that he is carrying his love for you when he leaves you, like a lucky penny. You and I will always have this love that we created together."

The smile returned to her round little face. "I really like that, and I can feel that love already." With that, the little girl hugged Olivia again. Both parts of Olivia were overflowing with love.

As Olivia opened her eyes, she could still feel the love she had for that younger part of her. She took a deep breath and sat in the love that filled every nook and cranny of her heart. She could feel it in every cell of her body. The harmonizing was happening. Olivia thought about her statement, "My heart is filled with love, and I know it so well that I can recognize the same love in you." Her heart was filled with love, and she was beginning to believe that she would know it well enough that she could recognize it in someone else. She recognized it in the younger part of herself, and that was a start. She had shifted out of her hidden, inner wounding, and now she was in her own kayak headed downstream.

Olivia's journey is just one individual way the phases can happen. When you take the journey into your own story, the manifestation of the phases will be different, but the phases will be the same. Let's review the five phases for calming the troubled water of having two people in one kayak.

A. Identify the other person in your kayak and the statement that brought you there.

B. Find the contrast.

C. Shift the statement and reposition your kayak.

D. Gather the information by finding the root of the statement, and identify the first time you felt it manifest in your life.

E. Embrace the information and harmonize your heart by going back to the first time you remember it being part of your story, then shift your statement for yourself in that time.

Once you have navigated through these phases, you will find that you can head downstream with ease. Be patient with yourself as you move through the steps. The freedom you will find on the other end is worth the time you may spend gathering and navigating your way back to your kayak.

The next troubled water scenario for you to examine is Paddling Upstream. As you walk through the steps and examples for getting out of this troubled water, remember, the goal is to practice the principle until it is second nature. Once you practice the principle, it will be easier to apply it to your story. Remember, if the examples bring up too much information or don't resonate with you, just be patient and tender with yourself and continue reading and exploring. A brilliant downstream flow in your life is just a turn of your boat away.

Example Two: Trouble in the Water
Paddling Upstream

THE SECOND SCENARIO IN WHICH YOU ENCOUNTER TROUBLE in the water is when you paddle upstream. Before focusing on another example of trouble in the water, let's revisit the sensation of a downstream-flowing movement.

Take a moment and call on a cellular memory in which you felt what it was like to be in perfect synchronicity with all that was around you. Like gears of a clock moving in perfect time, you engaged with people and events in your story. Feel the current of your life flowing downstream. Take a deep breath as you bask in the sunshine while the boat and current move together downstream. From here, let's look at the contrast of paddling upstream.

Paddling upstream is literally the opposite of flowing downstream. This is a contrast in direction and energy. When paddling upstream, you are in your kayak, but you are fighting, working, and struggling against the current. You can feel your paddle hitting the water and your muscles straining as you pull the paddle through the water. At first, you might feel strong in this struggle, maybe even justified. You feel as if there is purpose in the fight. You know you can power through it. But as you repeatedly strike the water, you feel your arms getting tired, your back starts to cramp, and the constant effort begins to wear on you. The discomfort seeps into your body and challenge plagues your mind. From here, happiness seems far away. The water splashes into your kayak, and fatigue sets in. There is a part of you that doesn't want to struggle, but you don't know how to stop, or you feel that stopping would be admitting defeat.

What would happen if you just put your paddles back in your kayak? You might lose what you were fighting for, you might not get what you want, or you might miss out on something. These things are possible. Every "might" that runs through your mind could very well happen. The question is, can you enjoy something while struggling? Can you thrive in your life while you fight for survival against the current? Think about how human beings behave when they are struggling. They are often on edge, short-fused, and pessimistic about life or their circumstances. The focus required for a struggle leaves little room for happiness. You become more isolated when you paddle upstream because your attention is focused on the struggle. By paddling upstream, you are missing out on all the possibilities waiting downstream for you.

There are different degrees of paddling upstream. At times you may find yourself in a full-fledged upstream battle with the river of life. Other times you might get your boat turned around facing upstream, and then realize that you don't want to engage in the struggle that goes with moving in that direction. You may not paddle and struggle, but end up paralyzed, facing against the current, just holding your position. Or you may be facing downstream, but your paddles are in the water ready to fight at any moment. You may even have your paddles in the boat, but your hands are gripping the paddles in anticipation of the struggle.

There are many ways to wind up paddling upstream. It happens when your internal dialogue gets tangled up or when you react against your surroundings. Because individuals are such strong mirrors for our information, interacting with them can catapult you into an upstream position. If you can recognize that you are paddling upstream, you can turn the kayak around and use the information to clean up your heart and find harmony within yourself.

There are endless versions of the "Paddling Upstream" inner dialogue. For every upstream inner dialogue that presents itself in your story, you get the opportunity to find the information that can lead you to your heart's harmonization and personal freedom. By finding and shifting the upstream paddling to a downstream movement, you will be able to give your tired heart a rest. Just as your arms would hurt and get tired from feverishly paddling upstream, your heart gets tired from going against the natural flow of your life. Let's see if any of these examples sound familiar or resonate with what surfaces in your dialogue.

I am so stressed about this that I cannot concentrate on anything else.

I am struggling or am irritated with . . .
 this person
 this job
 my situation

I am worried that I am going to miss out on . . .
 the things that I want in my life
 my mate
 this job
 happiness
 love

I have tried so hard to . . .
 keep my family happy
 make the right decisions
 find the right partner

I am so worried that . . .
    I am not a good enough parent
    I will never . . .

I am stressed out about . . .

I have to make . . . happen.

What happens if I can't make . . . work?

Where do I go from here?

When you use the phrases; "I should," "I have to," or "it has to be," you will almost always find yourself upstream. If you find these words: *worry, stress, struggle, irritation, anxiety, disappointment, frustration, annoyance,* sneaking into your vocabulary, then you will almost always find your kayak facing upstream. When you are in this position, separation from your heart and happiness are not far off. There are people who live the majority of their lives struggling upstream. I am sure you have come across them. These people can't find happiness even when it is right in front of them. They believe that everything needs to be a fight. Unfortunately, the more you fight against the current of life, the farther away happiness and harmony will be. You could survive like this, but the question you must keep in mind is, "Do I want to just survive my life, or do I want to thrive in it?" This principle will bring happiness back into reach. It starts with putting the paddles back in the boat and letting your kayak head downstream.

If you spend enough time paddling upstream, flowing downstream may feel foreign to you. When you are floating downstream, you are not reacting to or judging yourself or others. This lack of reaction and judgment may feel like inaction at first, but when you're in the downstream flow, you are interacting instead of reacting. Action is present, but it is focused inward, not outward. The action you are taking lies in consciously changing the direction of your kayak—consciously pulling your paddles out of the water. The action is in moving through the phase to keep yourself in your kayak and headed downstream. Why continue to struggle and fight against your own harmony? Why be a stranger to your own story? Take internal action, pull in those paddles, turn around, and embrace your story. Then, you will find your happiness and begin to live into it fully.

Utilizing the information associated with paddling upstream is similar to dealing with having two people in one boat. Let's start by adjusting the phases A through E to address paddling upstream. Phase A will identify the information or situation that made you want to put your paddles in the water and head in the wrong direction. In phase B we will look for the contrast between the effort of paddling upstream versus effortlessly floating along with the current of life. Once the contrast is created, you can then move on to phase C where you consciously shift the statement that turned your kayak against the current of your life. As you change your statement, you shift your kayak's position. When you are settled back into facing downstream, you can move into phase D in which you navigate to a place where you can gather the information. Then finally, you move to phase E where you embrace that information and harmonize your heart to the place where you can be brilliantly connected. In this place, you will be fully engaged in your story and continuing along with the natural current of your life.

Taking a closer look at your "upstream versus downstream" inner dialogue will help you understand how you can move through these phases. In our example we use the statement: "I am irritated and struggling with this person." This is a typical upstream statement because it is so easy to get swept up in negative circumstances with others. This statement could reflect the irritation you have with yourself, a family member, a person at work, a friend, a lover, or even a stranger. The words "irritated" and "struggle" can also be interchanged with stronger words that represent the upstream struggle. The dialogue may initially feel as insignificant as if it had come from an interaction with a stranger. However, if coming from a partner, parent, child, sibling, or co-worker, it may feel very significant.

Let's take a look at the outline again:

Step 1: **Embracing Life Downstream**

Step 2: **Identifying Trouble in the Water**
Two People, One Kayak
Paddling Upstream
Out of Your Kayak

Step 3: **Navigating Through the Information**
Phase A: Identifying Your Statement

Phase B: Creating and Acknowledging Contrast
Phase C: Shifting Your Statement Consciously
Phase D: Gathering Information
- *Identify the essence behind your identified statement*
- *Identify the first time in your life when you experienced that essence*
- *Find the root of the information*
- *Identify the old pile of information where it initiated*

Phase E: Embracing Information to Harmonize Your Heart
- *Go back to the first time you felt that essence and shift your statement there*

In phase A, identify the statement and the essence behind the statement that drew you into the upstream battle. Anytime you feel the sensation of pushing or fighting welling up within yourself, it's a great indicator that your paddles may be entering the water. This doesn't mean that you can't step outside of your comfort zone and try new things, or move forward in your personal evolution. It just means you should focus your conscious attention on how you do it. When you begin to fight or push against a person, situation, or even yourself, you are pushing against the current of your life and heart. When you begin to feel that sensation, visualize your kayak and acknowledge your paddles in the water. If the pushing or fighting against the circumstance gets stronger, then visualize yourself paddling harder. If the fight or frustration grows, then visualize your fight against your own current getting more feverish. This will help you identify and begin to understand that the fight and frustration has less to do with the other person and more to do with you. You may be frustrated with another person and their behavior, but it's your kayak and your river of life, so if you choose to engage in the dialogue, then it's your information.

The challenge when dealing with a frustrating situation is to separate the wrong that you believe yourself to be going through from the information or essence behind the situation. If you can begin to see that it is your story and your information—that it is more about you than the other person—then you will have a better chance of finding the essence behind the struggle. If you want to live a life of happiness, fully engaged in your story, embracing the freedom and harmony within your heart, then consider looking at all of the information that comes into your life with tender curiosity. This includes the upstream struggle. After you identify the statement, "I am irritated and struggling with this person," acknowledge that the irritation and frustration have less to do with them and more to do with you. Look at all the information that comes into your life as yours. It is there for you because it is your story, your river, your kayak, your heart, and your happiness. Remember everything that comes into your life is there to help you, not harm you.

As you interact with people, you are calling them into your space for a reason. The situation may be positive or negative, but it's there to help you if you choose to use it. We call in people and situations for many reasons and one reason is to help us see where our hearts want to heal. When someone comes into your dialogue, he or she is mirroring back to you something from within yourself. Sometimes this information can be used to reinforce that you are beautifully settled in your kayak floating downstream. Sometimes the information being mirrored to you reveals a struggle showing that you are paddling upstream. This allows you to see where you need to focus your conscious attention. So, if you find yourself frustrated or irritated with a person, identify what it is within the situation or person that frustrates you. Then you can use that knowledge as a mirror to show you what you need to do to head back downstream.

Phase B is where you create contrast. You look at your paddling upstream scenario and explore the contrast between it and floating downstream in your own kayak. By contemplating both the upstream situation and the downstream ideal, you can begin to appreciate the contrast. Look for the contrast by altering your statement. Change it to reflect the contrast. The upstream statement might blame others for the situation. For example, "Something you are doing is causing me to fight against the current of my life." Changing this to a downstream statement might sound like, "Something in this situation is calling up information that I can use to harmonize my heart so I can feel more free within my story." The downstream statement reflects your engagement in your story. Upstream points to someone else: "If you were not like this, or doing this, then I could be happy and not frustrated." Downstream interaction points to your own heart: "You are mirroring something within me that is longing to be shifted, and, if I can find it, then I can be happy and not frustrated." If you can see the other person as a gift rather than an adversary, then you are well on your way to creating contrast. Upstream dialogue says, "You are the problem that stands in the way in my life and story." Downstream dialogue says, "You are a gift, given to me so that I can identify and navigate my way through my life and story." Look for the contrast. Upstream holds the negativity and frustration of the situation and hands the power to relieve it to someone else. Downstream releases the negativity and frustration of the situation by taking responsibility for your own freedom within your story.

By creating contrast, you can see that you have a choice in how you perceive the situation. When you choose to fight against something over which you have little control like a person and their behavior, you will never be able to paddle away from it. The upstream battle is one that you can never really win. However, if you choose to use the situation as information for your story, then you can get your kayak headed back downstream by releasing old information in your heart and attaining harmony within yourself and with your story. As you wholly embrace this choice, you are fully appreciating the contrast in the situation.

Up to this point, you have identified the person and statement that created the trouble in the water. You found contrast from the statement. Now it's time to move toward changing the statement and repositioning your kayak, gathering and embracing the information to harmonize your heart and move downstream.

Moving to phase C, you change the statement. Changing the identified statement allows you to realize the possibility of changing the outcome. By changing your statement, you are creating an intention for yourself to shift into your own happiness and harmony. You want to create a statement that gives you room to engage in your story without struggle and irritation. When working in the area of paddling upstream, you want the new statement to cut through the struggle and create space and opportunity for freedom within yourself. Start with the original statement "I am irritated and struggling with this person." Then shift from irritation to gratitude. "I am grateful." Once the gratitude is there, add what the person mirrored to you. "I am grateful for the information that was mirrored to me." The more specific you can be about what the information was, the more useful it will be to you—this will be accomplished in phase D. From there, create movement downstream, "I am grateful for the *specific* information that was mirrored to me, and I will use it as my own." Think about how you might use it. This gives your new statement even more teeth. (We will discuss this more in phase E.) The new statement releases you from the struggle and irritation. It allows you to embrace the contrast that was created, and now you can move forward with the information. You can be active in your information and use it productively. Now that the statement has changed, your energy can shift from endless paddling against the current, to productively moving through your information to happiness and harmony. This leads you to phase D. With your kayak once again facing downstream, you are ready to gather the information from the situation to make sure you don't get caught paddling upstream against the same current of information.

In phase D, you are able to gather the information that you need to fully embrace your new statement as truth. You may already feel some freedom within your heart since you are facing back downstream, but remember phases D and E are where you begin fully engaging in your story. Your full freedom from this particular struggle is just around the corner, but first you must become conscious of the information. Think of the next phase as moving the freedom you attained from the head to the heart. Once you have harmonized the situation, you can begin embracing your joy. Gathering the information includes finding the underlying essence behind your initially identified statement and uncovering the first time you encountered that essence in your story. After you have the information, you can embrace it fully and use it to harmonize your heart.

The underlying essence behind the statement "I am irritated and struggling with this person" has endless possibilities because your emotions and information have endless possibilities. This is where being specific within that statement is important. As you look at what frustrates you about the other person or situation, you can use them as a mirror to find the essence behind this particular situation. If you are frustrated with someone because they are wasting your time, then that is the essence behind the frustration. Look to see where you feel that you are wasting time in your life, somehow. If you are irritated because someone is combative when they interact with you, then you look to see where you feel that combative pressure within your story. Once you've looked into the mirror of the other person, then gently look within yourself to see where that frustration resonates within your heart. The essence behind the frustration may be a little hard to see at first, but just be tender with yourself and keep looking. Describing what the situation feels like can help you isolate the essence. Is there a statement that you keep repeating to yourself in response to the situation? That statement can help you figure out what the underlying essence of the situation might be.

Once the essence is identified, you can determine the first time you felt it come up in your story. Your heart called in the information because it wanted to release it. If you can go back to the first time you recall engaging in the essence of the information, then you can work toward navigating through it to a place where it has little or no pull on your heart. This is where the statement shifts from your mind to your heart. This leads you to phase E, embracing the information.

Embracing the information in phase E allows you to harmonize your heart. Start embracing the information by revisiting your changed statement. "I am grateful for the information that was mirrored to me and I will use it as my own." From there, make it more specific to your story by applying the underlying essence. Remember there are endless possibilities for the essence behind the statement. Be curious with your story and look to see what comes up naturally. If the underlying essence was about wasting time, (as in one of our earlier examples), then you could make it more specific by saying "I am grateful to see the place where I feel like I am wasting time and how that separates me from what I want. I can now work toward what I want, fully engaged in my story." Once you clarify your statement, you can tap into the *you* from that initial recognition and make contact. When you go back and make contact, you are freeing the part of your heart that was stuck reacting to old information. Once you harmonize the part of your heart that was holding the initial wound, your new statement becomes truth for yourself.

Emma's Story: Paddling Upstream

LET'S WALK THROUGH THE PHASES WITH EMMA. Emma's trouble in the water is paddling upstream. Emma is a woman who has recently started becoming more conscious of all of the information around her. She has worked for the same company for a long time. One evening she returned home from the office all worked up. Her blood pressure was high and she could not wait to get on the phone to her friend and share the story about how crazy her co-worker Smith was. She knew that she would feel better if she could just tell someone and get confirmation about how crazy he was. Smith was generally likeable enough, but over the last couple of days he had been nasty to her. Every time they had interacted, his whole demeanor had been sour, and he had tried to shoot down every idea she had. She felt like she was going up against him every time they had an encounter. She knew her job, and she did it well. She wondered why he was second-guessing her. In fact, he was not her boss or even part of the project team she was on at the moment. Smith was usually a nice enough person, but this was just too much. They didn't always speak the "same language," or see eye to eye, but that had never been a problem before. She was so irritated and frustrated with him she could hardly stand it.

Some people hear a story like Emma's and their instinct is to cheer her on as she paddles upstream. After all, Emma's being wronged. This Smith guy needs to pull himself together and back off. Well, the statement "Treat me a certain way so that I can be happy," not only turns the boat upstream, but it also puts you in someone else's kayak. When you say, "I am frustrated with your behavior, and you should change, so I can be happy," you are fully engaged in paddling against the current.

Emma sat for a moment and thought about the information. She knew that she was paddling upstream with Smith, but she didn't have the time to deal with analyzing the situation while she was at work. She also knew that if she got on the phone and relived the information, she might feel better for a little while, but she would still wind up pushing against him the next day. If she wanted to stop pushing against him and paddling upstream, she was going to have to look at the information differently. Emma began moving through the phases.

Phase A was a breeze, she recognized her statement "I am irritated and struggling with Smith." (It was the same one we used in some of our earlier examples). She took a deep breath and started to create some contrast for herself. Her first step to find the contrast was the realization: "Damn you, Smith, you are a gift, not an irritation." She said it out loud, only half believing what she was saying. She laughed a little. It sounded pretty silly, and the laughter felt pretty good. "Smith, you are mirroring something within me that is longing to be shifted, and if I can find it, then I can be happy and not frustrated," she said sarcastically. It was hard for her to let go of the hurt just beneath the frustration. "If I let go of the paddles or frustration, then he will be getting away with treating me like crap," she thought. She took another breath and closed her eyes. She pictured herself in her kayak. She didn't want to paddle upstream. She was conscious enough to know that she felt better in her life when she was flowing along with the current instead of against it. "Okay, okay, I can do this," she said out loud. "I have to get my boat turned around." She knew that she needed to recall a positive moment in her life if she was going to get the boat turned around.

She took another deep breath and thought about the first time she and her sister visited the ocean by themselves. It was summer and her sister had just gotten her license. They had been given permission to take the car down to the ocean for the afternoon. It was warm outside, and she remembered grabbing her sister's hand and running along the water. The sand and water were kicking up around them as they ran together. She could see it and feel it. The two of them were laughing so hard. She felt so free and so happy. She could smell the salt in the air. As she took in another deep breath, she could feel her heart release. The corners of her mouth were turned up as every cell of her body remembered that beautiful moment when she was in perfect unison with everything around her. Emma found herself back in her kayak facing downstream with a full heart. "Okay, Smith, it's not about you, it's about me. Thank you for helping me find whatever this thing is that I need to shift." This time she meant it. With her kayak facing back downstream, she could move on to the next phase.

Emma had moved through phases A and B, identifying the statement and creating contrast. It did not take much time to get there, but it did take her finding a cellular memory to help her engage in creating contrast. Next, she needed to move through phase C, shifting her statement. Now that she was facing downstream, she could begin to shift the statement more easily. She could let Smith just be Smith. His information was for him; and now, what she had felt while she interacted with him was her information. "My new statement is, *I am grateful to have this information that was mirrored to me, and I will find the root of my frustration and release it so I can experience more freedom in my own story.*" She said it out loud as she wrote the new statement down on a sticky note. "Thank you, Smith," she said with a smile, this time meaning it.

She started to feel good about navigating through her own information. She was ready to gather the information in phase D. She could take her time and engage in her story with tender curiosity as she moved through the next phase. She began to think about the essence behind her interaction with Smith. When he kept coming at her with, "No, that's not right," and "We can't do that," she felt like he was being confrontational. Every time she said anything, he spouted out something that made her feel like he was "putting her in her place." He was being so combative. The word *combative* reminded her of something.

Earlier that week, Emma's brother had a birthday dinner at his house. Emma and her sister-in-law cooked all afternoon. They even made his favorite cake. Their sister was going to come over and join them for dinner, but before she got there, her brother seemed to grow more and more anxious. By the time they all sat down for dinner, she could tell something was not quite right with him. He brought up politics, a subject they all had differing opinions on and usually stayed away from. Once he was done with that subject, he swiftly moved on to yet another touchy subject, religion. She wondered why he was picking a fight with them on his birthday. Just like Smith, he was being combative. With her brother, it was easier for Emma to stay in her kayak facing downstream. She knew that her hands were reaching for the paddles, but she consciously chose not to engage in that struggle because she didn't want to cause heartache on her brother's birthday. She just let him do his thing; it was, after all, his birthday. After that night, she hadn't thought much about it until the word *combative* came up with Smith. Her heart really was calling in some consistent information.

The way the word *combative* resonated with her and brought up an incident from only a few days before helped her zero in on finding the essence of the information. She thought about Smith again. That combative feeling of pushing your opinion on someone else, as if it were the only way, felt oddly familiar to her. Being emotionally combative was the common thread in the situations she was calling in, so it must be related to the essence. The original statement, "I am irritated and struggling with Smith," was not about Smith but about the combativeness in the interaction. The next step was going back to the first time she could remember feeling that combativeness in her life. She loved her family very much, but they all had different ideas about what a happy life should look like. Her siblings were all married and working toward building their families. Her parents, who had been married to each other for almost forty years, expected her to follow along the same path as her siblings. She would go out on blind dates with men that her siblings set her up with and would be disappointed to find that they were a perfect match for the sibling, but not for her. Didn't her family know her at all? Did she have to sit across from another uptight suit that couldn't care less about the things she was interested in? As she thought about this information, she could feel that combative energy beginning to well up within her. She was on the right track. She could feel her heart trying to fight against all of the things that her family was trying to push on her. She reached back even farther into her memory.

She came to recall a moment of such bitter frustration that it almost turned her stomach and made her want to scream and fight against the unjustness she had felt. As she began to remember how that horrible day had played out, she was stunned to realize that she had not addressed this hurt before. She was seventeen. She had been sitting on her bed doing homework. As a versatile and well-rounded student, she was involved in the school newspaper and took art classes, but also excelled in math and history. She had gotten good grades and been friends with people in almost every group in the school. She loved writing and her dream was to move out of the northeast and go to school on the west coast where it was warmer, where she would study to be a writer. She had it all planned out in her mind. The applications were mailed out, and she had been waiting to hear back about acceptances to see what her options would be. On this day, her mother came into her room and sat at the edge of her bed. She seemed to be her cool-and-collected self, but she didn't say anything. Emma remembered taking her headphones off and looking at her mother. She noticed that she had the mail in her lap and was tracing the outline of the large envelopes with her manicured fingers. Emma now remembered the conversation as if it were yesterday.

"Mom, did I get any mail?"

Her mother turned to face her. "You did, Emma, and we need to have a chat about your future."

"My future," Emma had said with a smile, thinking about the possibilities her life could hold.

"Yes Emma, your future. Your father and I have been talking, and we believe that you should stay in New York and go to business school. We have thought long and hard about it and believe it is the right thing for you to do."

"What are you talking about? You know I want to go to California and study to be a writer. It's what I have been planning, and it's what I want to do," Emma argued.

"You can't be a writer Emma, it's not a stable market, and you can't waste time going to college studying something you can't use later. Your father and I have let it go too far. We should not have let you apply to these schools. Now the letters are in, and by the looks of the packets you probably got in."

"I got in? Let me see the letters."

Emma's mother handed her the two large envelopes. "Don't open them, Emma," her mother requested. "You are not going to go to those schools, Emma. You are going to go to Brown, just like the rest of the family has done. You can study English if you must, but you are not going to those schools, Emma."

"Why not, Mother? I don't understand. I researched the programs, and I know what I want to do."

"Well, young lady, your father and I know what we want for you as well, and I believe we know what's right for you. You will go to Brown, and you will see that it is the right choice for you."

She remembered how frustrating it was to talk to her mother. "And if I don't go to Brown, then what?"

"I am going to say this one more time, Emma. We are paying for you to go to Brown. You will go, and get your degree, and find a great job somewhere. We will not be supporting you in other endeavors. Do you understand?"

"But, Mother, I know I can—" Emma was cut off.

"Do you understand me, Emma?"

Devastated and stunned, Emma nodded her head and looked down at the envelopes in her hands. Not sure if she had it in her to fight, she sat feeling her heart rip at the seams. She could try to fight against her parents and break free, but, what if she failed and her parents were no longer there for her? She would have fought and failed, and she would have lost her parents' love, too. She could not bear to lose her dream and her family.

Her mother walked to the door and turned around to look at Emma, "Your father and I love you, Emma, and we only want what is best for you."

Emma watched her mother as she shut the door behind her. She curled up on her bed with the envelopes clutched in her arms. As tears fell down her cheeks, her heart was absorbing the wound that had just been created. To protect herself, she separated a little from her heart's center.

Emma ended up studying at Brown. She loved being in college and graduated with honors. She did as well in college as she had done in high school. She enjoyed her professors and classes. When she graduated, her family cheered her on as she walked across the stage. They threw her a big graduation party, and in many ways she lived as if the wound in her heart was not there. Emma thought about her business writing and how she was able to use that kind of writing to help people by writing grant applications. For Emma, every day is filled with writing and helping all sorts of people and groups. She truly loves the work that she does. There is not a day that goes by that she does not get to be productive and creative. She thought about that for a moment. She took a deep breath and tried to pull back to see it all as her brilliant information.

It was almost as if she had pushed the incident with her mother aside so that she could survive what she needed to do in her life. Emma thought back and noticed that every time her family pushed something on her, a part of her got fired up and wanted to push back, whether it was about the men she dated or something as simple as what they were having for a holiday dinner. The wounded part of her heart whispered to her to engage in combat the way she hadn't all those years ago.

The information was definitely less about Smith and more about her. All she needed to do was pay attention to what her heart was calling in. The wound that her heart was trying to heal was the one that was created on that day in her room with her mother. She could look back over the years since then and see where her heart had called in the information, but she had not yet been in a place to move through it. She remembered to be tender with herself and just appreciate the information she had gathered.

Emma made herself a cup of tea and moved to the couch. She thought about her new statement, "I am grateful to have this information mirrored to me, and I will find the root of my frustration and release it, so I can experience more freedom and harmony within my story." It was time for her to embrace the information so that she could find the harmony in her new statement.

"How do I shift my statement back to when I was seventeen?" she wondered. She thought about the girl sitting on the bed listening to her music. She was so happy. There was a large bay window in her childhood bedroom. Emma decided she would close her eyes and take herself back to the bedroom and sit in it, and watch the event unfold. Her present self snuggled up in the corner of the couch and closed her eyes. She pictured herself curled up in the bay window of that childhood room. She watched the seventeen-year-old lying on her bed, staring up at the ceiling. Watching the younger version of herself made her smile. She paid attention to some of the details of what she looked like. Her fluffy strawberry bangs and her oversized T-shirt. She took it all in and laughed to herself a little.

She noticed the door opening and looked over to see her mother standing in the doorway. She looked so young. She had not really ever thought of her mother as old, but she looked so much younger standing there with the envelopes in her hands. She watched herself sit up on the bed and take off the earphones. The Emma sitting in the window couldn't really make out all that they were saying, but she could see what was going on in a way that she couldn't all those years ago. She could sense what they were each feeling as they sat and interacted on the bed. She watched the excitement on her face wash away. She could not only see the confusion in her eyes, but she could feel it welling up in her throat and turning into frustration. She watched her young strong body shrink farther down, as if every cell was being weakened by her mother's words. She watched her mother closely. She had not noticed it before, but her mother seemed nervous. She looked down at her hands more than at Emma. She wondered if her mother could see what Emma saw as she sat in the window. She wondered if she could see that young girl sitting in front of her, melting away in pain. She might not have. It was almost as if her mother was pushing through something, not even seeing Emma. The Emma in the window seat watched as her mother walked to the door. As her mother turned around, she noticed something for the first time. Her mother's eyes were filled with pain. She didn't know if it was her mother's own pain or if it was pain she felt for her daughter. She watched her mother's lips move, saying that she loved her, and then the door closed.

As the Emma on the bed curled up and cried, the Emma in the window seat thought for a moment. She was startled by what she had seen in her mother and the questions that circled around her. She reminded herself that this was *her* story and *her* information. Not only was the situation not about Smith, it was not about her mother either. She may never really know her mother's story. How could she? She was just starting to know her own. With that thought, she knew it was time to make contact so that she could shift the statement for the girl lying on the bed. She thought about what it was that the crying girl needed. Because that girl on the bed was her, she was the only one who really knew how to ease the pain and heal the wound.

Emma stood up from the window seat and walked over to the bed. She pulled out the footstool that was tucked under the bed and sat down. Then, she reached out her hand and moved the strawberry colored hair out of the tear streams on the girl's cheek.

"Hello," she said tenderly to the girl on the bed. The girl looked up at her. Her big blue eyes were red and filled with tears. After a moment, the girl closed her eyes as if she just couldn't take any more pain. Emma took the girl's hands and held on to them.

"I am here to help you," she whispered, moving closer to the girl.

The younger Emma opened her eyes again. "To help me?" she whispered back.

"Yes, to help you. Do you think you could talk to me for a little while?"

"I guess so. What are you here to talk to me about?" she asked, with a sniffle.

"Well, I want to talk to you about what just happened with your mother." She paused to make sure the younger version of herself was following.

"I want you to know that it's okay not to fight. I know you feel like you have to choose between having the love of your family and fighting against them for what you want. I also know the frustration and pain that goes along with fighting for yourself and all that you are feeling." Emma told the girl.

"I didn't stand up for myself. Why can't I fight for what I want? I should have been strong enough to tell her, or make her see that going out to California is what I want," she said as she wiped her eyes.

Emma moved onto the bed and comforted the girl by stroking her hair. "What would you say if I told you that you don't have to fight to get what you want?"

The girl looked up at her, then sat up. "What do you mean?" she asked, with a confused look on her face.

"In your heart, you want to write and you want to help people. Am I right?" Emma asked, as she looked into the girl's eyes.

"That's true," the girl answered.

"If you want to write, then go to Brown and learn to write so that you can help people," Emma said.

"But, what about California?" the girl asked, hopelessly.

"One of your gifts in life is that you are able to make any place that you go, and any situation that comes up, work for you. You will thrive wherever you are," Emma said to the girl.

"How can I thrive if I can't even stand up for myself?" the girl asked in a frustrated tone. "Go to Brown and learn to write? Am I suppose to just give up on California?" she asked, still frustrated.

"It's not about giving up on California; it's about letting go of the feeling that you need to fight or you will lose something. You can embrace what you want without the fight or the disappointment," Emma said.

"How is that even possible?" young Emma asked.

"You said you want to write and help people, and you also want to go out to California. Which is more important to you right now?" she asked.

"I guess learning to write and helping people," she replied.

"Okay, then do it. Embrace it fully with your whole heart. Once you have done it, then you can revisit going to California," Emma said.

"Well, that does make some sense," the girl said, her brow still furrowed. Emma could feel the frustration starting to calm inside the girl.

"Do you still feel the urge to fight?" older Emma asked.

"Yes," she said with a deep breath.

"That feeling will haunt you if you can't figure out a way to move beyond it."

"It will haunt me?" the girl asked.

"Yes, it will. You may feel like you have to be on guard to fight all of the time. But, I am here to help you move beyond the feeling of needing to fight," she said.

"How?" she asked.

"Well, what if I told you that I am here to protect you, so that you don't have to fight? I am the part of you that is connected to your heart. I am the conscious you, who knows how to move through things without having to fight. Being in your heart-space is all the protection you need. And I promise you that I will always be there to help you navigate to that place where you can thrive. No matter what anyone says, you will always have someone to stand beside you and not only believe in you, but to support you each step of the way," Emma said, and the girl started to light up with hope and love.

"Actually, that does feel so much better. It feels like there is less pressure to prove something. Will you really always be there to help me?" the girl asked.

"Yes, I will. Always," Emma said with a smile. The girl smiled back.

"Now that you know you have me here with you, I want to tell you something about your family. It may help you interact with them later. You know, your mom and dad did the very best that they could in this situation. They are not making you go to Brown to hurt you. They are doing it out of love. They really think it is the right thing to do for you," Emma said.

"When do I get to decide what is the right thing for me?" the girl asked with curiosity.

"Emma, you just did. You decided that learning to write was the most important thing for you, even more important than fighting. You decided."

"Wow, the information and the facts are the same as when you first started talking, but if feels so different," she replied.

"I know—you get to move through it differently, with more freedom. I am very proud of you, Emma, you are truly an amazing person."

"Thank you so much for helping me," the teenage girl said as she hugged the woman sitting on her bed.

"I love you very much, Emma. Remember that I will always be there to help you," she whispered in her ear.

"I will remember."

Emma opened her eyes to find herself still sitting on the couch where she started. She took in a deep breath and felt the love and support all around her. The frustration and pull to fight was beginning to feel like an old memory. She could feel the harmony growing in every cell of her being. It was as if someone had hit a tuning fork and every vibration within her was in tune. Emma remembered her statement: "I am grateful to have this information mirrored to me, and I will find the root of my frustration and release it so I can experience more freedom in my own story." She was there. The statement was true. She was grateful for the information, and she had found the root of the frustration. It was hard for her to contain the joy she felt as she realized just how much more freedom she had gained from this new information. She had gone back to the hidden wound and shifted the information to heal it. She knew for sure that she was in her kayak and floating downstream; basking downstream was more like it.

Now, Emma could go to work the next day, and Smith could just be Smith. She no longer had to fight to prove anything to him. If something were to come up with him or anyone else, she would turn to that part of her that was always connected to her heart. She would not have to choose to fight and paddle upstream unless she wanted to. She thought about it again and realized it was the same with her family. They could be themselves, with their own opinions and ideas for her. The difference now was that she realized that she could choose and engage in her story the way she wanted to. As long as she was connected and in dialogue with the conscious part of herself, she would be just fine.

Now that you have read Emma's story, let's review the five phases that will help you stop paddling upstream and help you get your kayak turned around. First, you move through A—identify your statement that caused the trouble in the water. B—You find some contrast in the situation. C—You consciously shift the statement. D—You gather the information by finding the essence behind the statement. Then find the first time in your life that you felt that way. E—You embrace the information and harmonize your heart by going back to the first time you remember it being part of your story and shifting your statement there. Once you have navigated through all these phases, you will find that you truly have shifted the information, and your kayak will be floating downstream with ease. Remember to be patient with yourself as you move through these phases. The freedom you will find on the other end is worth the time you may spend gathering and navigating your way back to your kayak.

If you are working through information that looks similar to Emma's, I want to emphasize a couple of key points to keep in mind. First, the situation is not about the person or the thing that you are struggling against, it is about you. This small phrase can be tricky to accept because we live in a society that projects so much of our information onto others. Remember, this is the information that your heart is calling in. Use it for yourself and move toward focusing your mind inward rather than projecting outward. Second, be tender and curious with yourself as you move through the information. You have plenty of time, so try to relax into your story. As you work on phase E, in which you go back to the younger you and make contact, let go of any preconceived notions you have of how this should look. You may feel that it is silly or stupid to have to go back. As you experience this interaction, let go, and let your mind and heart feel and vividly picture that healing process. Move toward getting comfortable with the part of your heart that has been calling this information in. Your relationship with your story, your consciousness, and the things around you will slowly shift into a more harmonious space.

Now that you have looked into this example of paddling upstream you are well on the way to recognizing the information that can get you out of the trouble that you may encounter in the water of your life. Emma showed you how to put the paddles back in the kayak and stop paddling against the current, while Olivia showed you how to get back into your own kayak after being in someone else's. Now we will move on to the possibility of falling out of your kayak altogether. Andrew and Elizabeth will help you see how to get back into your kayak after being stranded in the water.

Example Three: Trouble in the Water
Being Out of Your Kayak

DEPRESSION AND ANXIETY ARE AN EPIDEMIC in our society. The feelings of hopelessness, agitation, restlessness, worthlessness, thoughts of suicide, overwhelming sadness—all of these things happen outside of your kayak. When you are living your life conscious and inside your kayak, you have a way to navigate through these emotions. From your boat, you can use these feelings as indicators that will help to guide you. Outside of your kayak, you don't have the ability to navigate through the information because you have to work so hard to survive. Have you ever tried to console a person who was so upset about something that there seemed to be nothing you could do that would help? You might get the impression that the person is unable to hear things you say, and that your efforts to console the person give little comfort. That is because when a person is outside of his or her kayak and in the depths of the water, the mind and heart are so focused on surviving that processing what you are saying may become impossible.

There are many ways that you can end up out of your kayak and floundering in the water. Maybe an old wound or old pattern that runs through your mind tossed you overboard. Maybe you abandoned your own kayak thinking that you would feel better in someone else's, but then you found yourself knocked out of the other person's kayak and thrown back into the water, unable to locate your own boat. If being in your kayak is being conscious, then being out of your kayak is being caught up in something that pulls you away from your consciousness. Maybe the thing that pulled you into the water is an addiction to something. As you fill your mind, body, and space with whatever consumes you, you also find that you are unable to stay in your kayak, and you are out of touch with your consciousness.

There are many other ways for the relationship between you and your kayak to manifest in relation to the water. At one end of the spectrum, you may find yourself lodged on a sandbar, calf-deep in water, holding on to your boat, but unwilling or unable get comfortable sitting in it floating downstream. Maybe your boat is floating in the water, but you are desperately clinging to the side, unable to find the leverage to pull yourself back inside. Another manifestation of this kind of trouble might have you seeing your boat ahead, but, as hard as you try to get closer, you find yourself drifting farther and farther from it. At the extreme end of the spectrum of possible situations, you might be so far out of your consciousness that you can't even find the location of your boat. You may be so lost in the water that there is no recognition of consciousness and your boat. In this case, you may find yourself barely keeping your head above the water. While in a constant state of struggling for survival, you splash about trying to stay afloat, but your head keeps going under, and you can't seem to catch your breath, let alone search for your boat that feels long gone.

Visualizing that far end of the spectrum, you can start to picture a scenario of being out of your kayak. You can imagine the feelings of desperation and frustration as your feet barely brush the bottom of the riverbed. Your body is fully immersed, and the water is getting in your mouth as you fight to keep your head up. The white water is swirling around till you can no longer feel the ground beneath you at all. As you pump your arms, your muscles burn and the current never slackens. When you are in this kind of anguish, stress and anxiety are unavoidable. The feelings of hopelessness and unworthiness add to the problem and can paralyze you in the water. Even if you struggle against those feelings, you might feel lost in them. As the water consumes your body, the negative emotion takes over your mind and heart. You close your eyes and the pain is still there. The tears you find yourself crying don't give you release or relief. In this space, you are separated from your consciousness.

No matter what end of the spectrum you find yourself, ankle deep in the water on the sandbar, or completely lost in the churning water—if you are in the water, there is information that your heart wants and needs you to move through. Moving through this information not only gets you back in your kayak, but it allows you to get to a deeper and freer place within your own story. It leads you to a place where your heart and consciousness are in complete harmony.

To get to the other side of the information, you must move through it, and if you are out of your kayak, the best place to start is by identifying where you are. This takes us right back to step two: identifying trouble in the water. Once you identify that you are out of your kayak and acknowledge the severity of the situation, you can move into step three: navigating through the information. Just as with the other two scenarios of trouble in the water, you navigate through the information using phases A through E to move you through the current information and the old information that it is linked to. In phase A, you identify the statement that got you where you are. In phase B, you create or acknowledge the contrast within the situation. In phase C, you consciously shift your statement. In phase D, you gather the information and get to the root of the old information that landed you in the water. In phase E, you embrace the information to harmonize your heart.

Let's look at what getting back into your kayak after being in the water looks like. Andrew and Elizabeth are going to help illustrate how to navigate through the information of being out of your kayak. First, let's meet Andrew. Andrew found himself so far out of his boat that he felt himself drowning in the water. Once we see how he was able to claim his story and use his information to get back into his kayak, we'll meet Elizabeth. We will explore how Elizabeth ended up in someone else's kayak and then found herself knocked into the water, struggling to find the way back to her own boat.

Andrew's Story: Not Knowing Where Your Kayak Is

ANDREW FOUND HIMSELF IN A PLACE where the volume of noise from his information had been continuously getting louder. He didn't just one day wake up to find that he was struggling against life. The struggle had been a slow and steady progression. There had been several times where he was painfully uncomfortable in his life, but inevitably the volume would go down and he would mange to survive his way through the chaos. Each time he survived a phase like this, he became a little more cynical and fundamentally a little less happy as a human being.

If you met Andrew, you would think he was a happy well-adjusted man with a beautiful family, successful business, and lots of wonderful friends. While he was outwardly known to stress about work, he was also fun to be around. When he was able to connect with people, he could see the joy and possibility in life. He listened to his friends and was a loving father and supportive husband. Overall, Andrew was a wonderful man who had achieved many different levels of success within his life. The only problem was that life always seemed a step out of reach for him. He had a hard time appreciating where he was because his mind was always a step ahead. Unable to be present, Andrew often found himself lost and just outside of all the wonderful things in his life. He built an incredible life and was surrounded by amazing people, but he found it hard to enjoy the life he had built. The times when he was able to stop pushing forward, all he could focus on was the struggle or fight that getting to that place had put him through.

Andrew's relationship with his kayak had been one where he started floating downstream, but he got lost in the reeds, so he got out of his boat and swam to a sandbar to take a breath. He would recover, then dive back in and swim to the next sandbar, paying little or no attention to his boat. It's not that he meant to be unconscious. He was actually very deliberate in many aspects of his life, but being deliberate and conscious are not exactly the same thing. His mind was sharp, and it allowed him to move through his life successfully, even without being conscious and in his boat. He knew how to manage his life. He learned exactly where and when to rest. Plus, he could hold on to the edge of his wife's kayak or find a sandbar that would allow him enough refuge from the chaos in the water to survive. But, that is exactly what he had been doing—*surviving* his life. He could have gone on surviving his life. His children were almost grown, and despite all the stress, his body had not yet given out on him. He could keep struggling to swim to the next thing in front of him, pushing and fighting the water around him, but he was getting tired. He could tell that the volume on his information was getting louder again. Andrew's heart was calling in blatant contrast, and it was turning up the volume on his information in hopes that he would clear out the old wound that was straining his heart and causing him to struggle.

For Andrew, *Phase B—Creating Contrast* came before *Phase A—Identifying Your Statement*. Before he could even see that there was a statement to find, the contrast had to build so that he could truly see the chasm between where he was and what he wanted. Because his mind was so sharp, his heart had taken a back seat for many years. It was only by creating contrast that he could awaken to the notion that a different way of living could be attained.

Before we hear more of Andrew's story, let's review *Phase B—Creating Contrast*, as it applies to the "being out of your kayak" variety of trouble in the water. We need to remember that we call in contrast so that we can more effectively see the difference between floating downstream, consciously engaged in our lives and in our kayaks, versus struggling and reacting to our lives, outside of our kayaks and having to fight the current to keep afloat. Think about the mirrors and reflections that we call into our lives. If we are out of our kayaks and struggling in the water, then the actual struggle can be your mirror, and seeing that will add a deeper layer to the contrast. If your heart is calling in the struggle and you keep finding yourself out of your kayak, then that contrast is where you find your information. In that contrast, you can discover the statement that will lead you right back to your boat.

If we take a deeper look at Andrew's contrast, we can see where his statement emerges. At this point in Andrew's story, we find him in a place where there is a mix of information. Several years prior, Andrew had started a magazine that had taken off and over the years had done well. Hiccups had arisen in the business, as always, but he had managed to survive the roller-coaster rides. During some of the easier years, he had returned to school and gotten his Ph.D. Even though it was hard to oversee the magazine, provide for his family, and deal with being a Ph.D. student, he seemed to thrive on the thrill of it all. There was a part of him that felt better when there were more balls in the air, and during that period of his life there were plenty.

Over time, Andrew found that his heart was no longer in the magazine business. He wanted to be done with it and had some options on the table for selling his company. He had also started to teach at a college in a neighboring city and was hoping to start guest lecturing at other colleges the following semester. His children were all healthy, and his wife was smart, beautiful, and completely engaging. On paper, his life was great. Things were lining up perfectly for him. But for some reason, all of the positive elements felt distant to him. As illustrated by the Stream–Kayak Principle, Andrew was caught in the water where all the details of life and all his challenges swirled around him. His mind kept replaying the challenges over and over again until the simple joys seemed far away. The conscious connection to his heart and story were in his kayak, which was caught in the reeds downstream. Even though all of his successes were a part of his story, he could not touch them or engage with them. All he seemed to be able to engage in was the struggle and fight to get things accomplished. His mind always sought out the places where things went wrong. He couldn't help but focus on what he didn't yet have and wanted to attain. He wondered how he could have gotten to a place in his life where everything felt so difficult. When had he become the grumpy old man standing in the back of the party watching, but not being able to participate in the fun?

For Andrew, the contrast of feeling miserable, in what should have been a brilliant life, manifested itself daily. The separation from his consciousness started to make him feel depressed. His frustrations with the details of life were growing and the volume was becoming so loud he couldn't help but seek relief. He tried to find solace in good food and wine, which would satiate him and bring him some comfort, but that comfort wouldn't last. He tried pushing the people in his life to change into what he needed them to be, but that only caused more confusion and frustration.

School, work, and his family were acting as mirrors for Andrew. One day it all came to a head, and the volume got so loud that he finally turned the information inward and began to see the old wound that the mirrors were reflecting within his heart and story. In school, the head of the program and the other professors were not providing Andrew's student team with the information they needed to be successful in their assignments and projects. Andrew found himself saying, "If they could just give us more information or pay attention to how much each professor is demanding of us, then the experience would be better." At work he found himself saying, "If they would just offer me more money, then I could easily sell the magazine." At home he found himself saying, "If you—my family members— could just communicate with me more, or pay more attention to me, our home life would be happier."

You can always tell that you are out of your boat when you try to get other people or situations to make you feel connected. If your focus is completely blurred, and your mind is lost in patterns that are only serving to cause frustration and breed the feeling of separation, then you are out of your kayak. If you are caught in an undertow of anxiety, or you find that fear is ruling how you react to the things in your life, then you are out of your boat and being taken over by the river of life. If you recognize these characteristics in yourself and your story, try to be tender with yourself and use the information around you to slowly bring awareness back to your heart and story. Just noticing the contrast, and seeing where you are in relation to your boat, brings you closer to harmony. As you begin to see the reflections of your heart, you can bring awareness to where you are in the river. You can use those reflections to focus your statement and navigate through your information. From there, you will find yourself getting closer and closer to your boat until you can step back into it comfortably. Getting back in your boat may be challenging, but your heart has called in everything that you will need to do it. Now it's up to you to utilize the information you have in your grasp to get back in your boat.

Andrew's heart had called in enough contrast for him to pay attention so he could move through phase B, creating and acknowledging contrast. Now that he was beginning to see the information around him as his own, his statement was starting to emerge. He could more effectively move through phase A, identifying his statement. As he looked back, he found himself projecting onto others. His awareness of that projection brought his statement to consciousness. "If they could just give us more information, or pay attention to how much each professor is demanding of us, then the experience would be better." "If they would just offer me more money, then I could easily let go and sell the magazine." "If my family members could just communicate with me more, or pay more attention to me, things would be better. I would feel better and our home life would be happier." He noticed the similarity in the statements. In each one, he wanted more: more information, more time, more attention, more money, and more communication. As he thought about these statements, he realized that the longing for more had driven him his whole life. The volume and contrast may have gotten louder over the last few years, and significantly louder over the last few months, but it had been there for a long time. The push to connect to more had always been a part of how he interacted with the world. As he curiously looked at all of the statements that were running through his mind, he was able to boil them down to one that felt like it held a lot of weight. "I have to push, fight, or search for more because what I want is always a little out of reach."

Now Andrew was prepared to move into the next phase and start to shift things for himself. Phase C is the place where you really start creating movement forward, toward your kayak and consciousness. In phase C you start to create a new intention for yourself by consciously shifting your statement. For Andrew, his original statement was all about separation, so his shifted statement became all about connection. The image and pattern that Andrew's mind kept replaying was one that showed him being separated from what he truly wanted. By changing the statement, he was able to take the first steps toward changing the pattern and image. A clear shifted statement provides a focal point that keeps you on track with your desired destination, your kayak. Your statement must illustrate a new consciousness and give you a tangible and applicable objective to interact with. In Andrew's circumstance, his shifted statement of connection kept him engaged, and focused on getting back into his boat by consciously choosing to direct his attention to connection.

Andrew's original statement could easily be shifted. It went from, "I have to push, fight, or search for more because what I want is always a little out of reach," to "Everything my heart wants is within reach because I am completely connected to all that I need and all that I want." This change allowed him to step out of a place of reaction and into a place of interaction. The shifted statement allowed him to have room to interact with his heart and information. Once Andrew had set his intention, he could work on making it a reality in his life by moving into phase D— Gathering the Information.

Phase D is where the work really gets juicy and you can start to feel the momentum of your action moving you forward to your kayak. Gathering information is the down and dirty "how to" part of this principle. It moves you deeper into your heart and story, allowing you to unlock your heart's freedom. If you can shift your statement in your *mind*, you know you are on the right track, but if you can shift your statement in your *heart*, you have made it back into your kayak where there is endless freedom.

As you move through phase D and gather your information, you will be looking at the essence—the hidden undercurrent—of your initial statement to find the root cause or wound that was created. You will scan the old piles of information that you have gathered to determine the first time that you felt that essence or undercurrent. Allow your mind and heart to open, and tenderly look to see where that feeling or undercurrent initially appears in your old piles. Don't worry about the accuracy of the memory. Healing comes from identifying and answering what your heart remembers and the wound that it has been carrying. Sometimes facts have little to do with piles of old information. Remember, it is less about the other people in the memory and more about you. Keep the focus on how you feel and what you are experiencing in the memory.

It wasn't hard for Andrew to find the initial wound. He had not consciously thought about that day in decades, but as he began to remember the situation, he could see how the events of that day had been quietly haunting him. He could feel how that undercurrent had been pulling at him, and how it had created an illusion of separation.

Andrew closed his eyes and the picture came to him immediately. He was about five or six, and it was a rainy Saturday. He and his sister had gone to dinner with their mother at a pizzeria not far from their house. Lately his mother hadn't been cooking as she usually did. She had been fighting a lot with his father, and she didn't seem to have the energy or patience to cook. At first Andrew thought that going out for dinner was a perk caused by the fighting, but it had gotten old quickly. The three of them sat quietly at the table in the pizzeria. Andrew and his sister ate their pizza while their mother barely sipped her soda. She had been too on edge to eat. On the ride over, the windshield wipers on their van had stopped working and, with the torrential rain, it created one more stress she had to deal with. After they finished eating, Andrew's mother stopped at the pay phone and called their father. He had spent the last two days somewhere else. Andrew and his sister had guessed that he was at their grandmother's house. Andrew could hear his mom's voice starting to rise, so he peeked around the corner and listened.

"I tried to wait it out, but I can't just keep the kids here, we need to get home. Just meet us there and fix it."

Andrew waited as his mom paused. He wished he could hear what his father was saying on the other end of the phone.

His mother stared up at the ceiling, "You said you would fix them the last time it rained and here we are once again. Just meet us at the house." Andrew heard the receiver slam down and saw his mother turn toward him.

"Let's go, kids," she said as she ushered them out through the rain and back into the van. Andrew remembered hearing the tick of the hazard lights as his mom drove home. The rain pounded heavily on the windshield, but the windshield wipers didn't work, so she drove slowly, trying desperately to keep them safe. Once they were home, Andrew and his sister turned on the TV and waited for their dad to come home. When he finally got there, he said hello to them and then followed their mother into the kitchen where they started arguing again. Andrew remembered wanting them to stop fighting, and this is where the wound of separation began. He let his mind continue to move forward through the memory. His dad went into the garage and worked on fixing the windshield wipers on the van. Andrew decided to go out and join him. It seemed quiet in the garage. His dad didn't say much to him, but it felt good to have him there.

When the van was fixed and the tools were put away, they went back into the house. His sister had gone up to her room, and as they walked through the kitchen, his mother asked him to go upstairs to his room, too. Within a couple of minutes, his parents were in a full-blown fight. Doors were slammed, and while he could not make out what was being said, he knew none of it was nice.

Andrew looked out the window and saw that his dad was loading up his trunk. He ran downstairs. He didn't see his mother, but he knew his dad was outside, so he quickly opened the front door to see if he could make out what was happening. The rain had slowed down to a drizzle, and he ran through the wet grass to the driveway where his father was moving things from the garage into his car.

"What are you doing, Daddy?" he said, almost begging for information.

"I'm sorry, Andrew," is all that he said, shaking his head. He kept saying it over and over. Andrew was so confused. What was he sorry for? He didn't understand. Andrew stood under the canopy of the garage as his dad opened the front door of the car and turned back to look at him. Their eyes met, and while Andrew was not sure about what was happening, he could feel his eyes starting to well up. His dad got into the car. As the door closed, the tears started to roll down Andrew's soft young cheeks. The car pulled out of the driveway. Before Andrew knew it, his legs were moving. That little six-year-old boy was running after the car. He was trying to chase it down, as if he could stop it or capture it somehow. He ran all the way to the end of the street before the car was out of sight.

As Andrew remembered that day, he could feel his eyes welling up just as they had while he had stood in the garage. He couldn't catch his dad that day, and the connection, love, and assurance that he had felt up until that point had vanished along with his dad into the distance. He had been trying to catch them and get them back ever since, but like the car on that rainy evening, they were always just out of reach.

The information had always been there. The old wound was buried among all the other information Andrew had gathered in his life. His mom had remarried shortly after that incident, and life had started to feel normal again for Andrew. The wound that was created that day now had scar tissue around it, preserving it. All the new information that came in had been filtered through that old wound, creating that feeling of disconnection. No matter how connected or loved Andrew was, the information would filter through the old wound and he would react to it as if he were disconnected. The old information kept him feeling like that boy at the end of the street, devastated because he could not catch the car and the love of the man in it.

Now that Andrew knew where that the old wound was, he could begin to feel himself getting closer to an even deeper truth. He was not exactly sure what it was, but for the first time in a long time he could feel that there was a thread of connection within him. This new information made him wonder about the connections that he had been able to create in his life. He pondered the relationships he shared with his wife and children. If he felt like he had been connecting in those areas when he was out of his boat, what would happen when he got closer to being in his kayak? The thread of connection that he was feeling would only get stronger as he embraced the information and harmonized his heart. This could only mean that his connection to his wife and children would grow and deepen.

Andrew needed to now step though phase D into phase E—embracing the information. This phase is all about going back to that first memory and creating the space to heal the old wound that is there. This is where the conscious you of today returns to the memory. As you go back to the memory, the conscious you of today makes contact with the part of you, or image of you, that got wounded. By making contact, you can begin to shift the wounded space. The conscious you of today can create a healthy dialogue with the younger you that is holding the wound. As you create this new and healthy dialogue around the wound, you may find that the wound starts to dissipate. Where there once was a feeling of confusion, now there may be a feeling of understanding. Where there once was a feeling of abandonment, there may now be a feeling of connection. The dialogue that you create within yourself can bring freedom and peace to the younger version of you and will inevitably bring freedom and peace to the present, conscious you of today. The brilliant part of creating this new dialogue is that the conscious you of today is the only person in the whole world who can know exactly what to say or how to interact with the wounded part of yourself to make it heal. You are the only person who knows the inner workings of your heart and all the information that it holds. You are the only one who can know what actually happened to create the wound, making you the only person who can really heal the wound.

Moving through phase E is all about truly seeing that wounded part of your heart and healing it. The most effective way to do this is to use your memory of the place where the wound was created. It is a tangible way of creating the shift and allowing healing to come into that wounded space. To do this, you first have to really look at and identify with that younger version of yourself. Make the interaction as tangible and alive as you can. Notice what you are wearing or how your hair looks. See if you can spot details that connect your mind, heart, and body to this image of yourself. Take note of your surroundings. Notice if you are inside or outside. The more you identify with your surrounding and with that image, the easier it will be to make contact and begin to communicate.

After you have recreated the situation, start to bring the conscious you into the picture. Close your eyes and get to a place where you can allow yourself the space to really picture the conscious you of today walking into the room, or up to the version of you that holds the wound. Make contact with yourself in as many ways as you can. Use your voice, body language, and eye contact. You can even physically interact with the wounded you. Start slowly if the situation calls for patience. Hug the younger you if he or she needs to be hugged. Pick the child up if he or she needs to be moved. Find what the child needs and provide it. Look into the child's eyes and say what his or her heart needs to hear. Talk, listen, and shed light, tenderness, compassion, and understanding into a dark and painful place. As you move through the conversation, see the understanding grow. Teach your former self that the *current you* is aware of what happened—that your love and presence will be constant, and that you are always there for your former self. From this point forward, you will be consciously engaged in your story so the younger you will never be alone or without information and understanding again. Your consciousness and your connection to your heart means that you will always be listening for what you need. As you identify with this part of yourself, you can create a dialogue that can be restarted anytime throughout the day. The initial contact can be like a meditation that you guide yourself through. Give yourself the space and time to really connect. Then, if you find yourself out of your kayak again, you can use that connection to help you find your way back. That younger image of you gives voice to the wounds of your heart. Once the dialogue is started, you have a tangible way of illustrating your struggle and longing so you can heal into your freedom. The younger you will always be there to help you identify with the old information that is causing the hiccups in your heart. This powerful tool can lead you toward finding harmony in your heart and story.

As Andrew started to move on to the next phase, he reminded himself of his intention and repeated his new statement to himself: "Everything my heart wants is right within reach because I am completely connected to all that I need and all that I want." This idea didn't seem as foreign as it had when he first came up with it. He closed his eyes, and with his intention set, he watched the images play out in front of him again. He saw the little boy at the pizzeria and in the car. He watched him sitting on the couch with his sister. He noticed the relief on the little boy's face as he heard his dad walk in the door. As he watched the little boy helping his dad with the windshield wipers, he noticed that the little boy's relief was now layers deeper. He recognized the little boy's hope and his feeling of connection to his dad, to his family, and to himself. He realized that this was the last time that he had felt that connected. Everything he needed was still within reach, and anything was still possible.

Andrew continued to watch the little boy go upstairs and look out the window. He felt him rush down the stairs and out into the rain. As he watched that final interaction with his father, Andrew again felt the welling up of emotion, but he saw something new this time, too. The pain in his father's face as he looked back at that young boy standing by the car surprised Andrew. Then, just like before, he heard the door close and saw the taillights on the car go red. Andrew could feel the desperation and confusion in the boy. He followed the boy as he sprinted to the end of the street. The pain in the boy's face was almost too much to bear and he could feel his heart ripping open all over again. It was there at the end of the street in the rain that he decided to make contact. He couldn't help himself. Being a father himself, he couldn't stand and watch this boy suffer.

Andrew walked up behind the crying boy, and put his arm on his shoulder, and squatted down beside him in the rain. He looked at that sweet little face and the tear-filled brown eyes and longed to make the world okay for him. The little boy looked right back at him. He had been screaming for his father the whole time he had been running down the street. As soon as the little boy felt the connection of the person squatting down beside him, he broke out into uncontrollable sobs. Andrew held him close and told him to cry as much as he wanted. He could tell the little boy was consumed by the separation. He decided to use a trick that he had used on his kids when they were young. He whispered into the little boy's ear, "You can scream if you want." He gave him permission to release in the biggest way that he could. The little boy's sobs slowed as he looked at Andrew, even more confused. "You can scream if you want. I will be right here. Just scream as loud as you can." The little boy wiped his eyes, threw his head back, and screamed from the core of all he was. Andrew knew that was exactly what he wished he could have done, and now a part of him had been able to do it.

Andrew looked into the boy's eyes and told him that they needed to get out of the rain. The boy shook his head.

"I don't want to go," he sobbed.

"It's okay, I will be with you. You won't be alone," Andrew said, as he picked the child up. The boy gripped on to him so tightly that it made Andrew hold him tighter right back. He walked into their backyard and maneuvered his way up into the tree house that his dad had built for him and his sister. He sat there on the floor for a long time with the boy in his lap, holding on to him with his head buried in his chest. Andrew knew that the boy was trying to figure it all out. This was the place where the chasing and disconnection started. He knew that this was the place he needed to heal if he wanted his new statement to become reality. So, he decided to talk to the child and help him figure it out.

Andrew patted the boy's back as he told him that he knew that he was in pain. He asked the little boy to tell him where it hurt the most. The little boy pulled back and looked at Andrew's face for a moment, then put his little fists up to his chest. "It hurts in my heart," he said, as he fought back more tears.

"I am so sorry," Andrew said.

The little boy started spouting questions. "Will I ever see him again? Did he leave because of me? How can I get him to come back?"

"I know this is hard for you, but I want you to listen to me very closely.

He did not leave because of you. We can't fully know why he had to go, but I saw him, and I could tell that it was hard for him to leave you," Andrew said.

"Then, why did he do it?"

"I'm sorry, but I don't know."

"Will he come back?"

"I'm afraid he won't come back in the way that you want him to."

"So I have lost him. I have lost my dad?" The boy started to cry again.

"Shhh, it's alright. It feels like you have lost everything, doesn't it?" he asked the boy.

"Yes it does," the little boy responded.

Andrew offered up a question, "What if we look at it a little differently?"

"What do you mean?"

"What if we look at a bigger picture? What if I told you that you had everything that you needed right in front of you? Even if your dad is not in that bigger picture for this moment, everything else is."

"I don't understand," the little boy said.

"Well, tell me all of the things that you are going to miss the most about your dad being here."

"I am going to miss him teaching me things and laughing with me. I am going to miss Friday dinners as a family. I felt safe—and *complete*—when he was here, and now that he is gone it feels like something is missing," the little boy said.

"Well," Andrew started. "What if I told you that you are going to get most of that back? One day not too far off, you will have someone to teach you things and make you laugh. You will feel safe again, too. And while your family will be a little different than it was before, it will feel complete again. Until that happens, and even after that happens, I will be right here with you. I will never, ever leave you."

"I don't understand," the boy replied. "My dad left me."

"I know, but I never will. All of the things that you want are right here for you. The love and connection—you have it. The safety is there. Soon, Friday night dinners will be back, and you will have a man in your life to teach you and show you everything that you need to know," Andrew told him.

"But even if another person comes into my life, what about the love I have for my dad?" he asked.

"That is a great question, and I am going to tell you something that not a lot of people know. The love that we create with people doesn't disappear."

"It doesn't?" the boy questioned, curiously.

"Nope it doesn't. We create love with people, and it ties us together. That love can go beyond time and space. It's kinda like the Force in Star Wars. You know how the Force is with you? Well, the love is with you too." Andrew put his hand on the little boy's chest in the place where he had said that it hurt earlier. "The love is in there, and I am right here for you. Everything your heart wants is right within reach because you are completely connected to all that you need and all that you want." Andrew was able to say his shifted statement to the boy, and it was true. His heart felt so much lighter. As he looked into the little boy's face, he could see the feeling of connection coming back. The little boy smiled at him. "I think that I like that," he said to Andrew.

"Me too," Andrew told him. Andrew hugged him again and felt his heart settling into harmony.

That push forward had shifted the old information to make more room for connection and harmony in Andrew's heart. Andrew had done it. He had embraced his information, and had shifted the old information, and healed the wound. His heart was completely connected to his story and he was back in his kayak floating downstream. From here, he could interact with the new information that came into his life and no longer had to react as new information hit up against the old wound. The wound had been shifted. The memory that was left no longer had any energy behind it and could now be exactly what it was, information there to help him evolve and find a deeper sense of harmony.

Elizabeth's Story: Getting Kicked Out of Someone Else's Kayak

ELIZABETH'S STORY ILLUSTRATES ANOTHER ASPECT of being out of your kayak. It shows us what it is like getting lost in the water, without your kayak, after being knocked out of someone else's boat; and what happens when you try to get back in your boat only to lose your balance and end up in the water again. For the first bit of this scenario, you might think back to Olivia's story. Finding yourself in someone else's kayak is very easy to do, but in the long run it's just not sustainable. Olivia was able to go from her fiancé's kayak directly back to her own, but the transition is not always that easy. Sometimes, when you find yourself in someone else's boat, you end up getting kicked out, which usually catches you off guard. When this happens, you usually can't find your own kayak right away, so you end up lost and struggling in the water. The second area of information that Elizabeth navigates through is struggling to get back into her own kayak. Unfortunately, like many people, once Elizabeth was able to find her kayak and climb back in, she lost her balance and fell right back in the water. Fortunately, she persevered and was able to get settled into her own boat and find harmony for her heart as she shifted more into the flow of her story.

Let's look at both parts of Elizabeth's story: first, where she is knocked out of her boyfriend's boat; and then, where she struggles to stay in her own boat. Look at the background information of Elizabeth's story. Then, take a deeper look at the inner dialogue that was created within these scenarios. This helps illustrate how she was able to navigate her way back to her kayak through consciousness and personal freedom.

When Elizabeth found herself struggling in the water, she was in her late twenties. She was an attractive and shy young woman who had overcome a lot of obstacles to accomplish things that she was proud of in her life. She put herself through college and managed to make great grades. Her education was followed by an internship, and then a high-paying job in her field. She had worked her way up from next to nothing, and had settled into a life that felt full. Two years prior to that period, she met a man who she felt "hung the moon." He was wonderful and supportive of all that she wanted to accomplish. Her family life had not been the best, and in many ways he seemed to have stepped in and made up for some of the love that she felt she had missed out on as a child. They became inseparable. They always had a wonderful time whenever they were together. The last two years had been filled with full weekends and adventurous vacations. They laughed and had fun together, even if they were just hanging out doing nothing special. On paper, things seemed to be going well.

What Elizabeth didn't realize was that, in many ways, her happiness had become dependent on her relationship. She worked so hard for so long, and when she started to date her boyfriend she felt like she could finally rest. He took such good care of her, and when they were together she felt safe and happy. In a way, she had taken a deep breath and fallen into him, or at least into his kayak. While, on the outside, the relationship seemed to be "peaches and cream," the reality of what was happening was a little bit different. Elizabeth had paddled upstream and had struggled with her own happiness and situation in life for a long time. When this man came along and offered up a space of playfulness, care, and love, she gladly jumped into his boat. She was willing to hand over her consciousness in exchange for the peace and joy that she found herself now experiencing.

When you are in someone else's kayak, it can start off feeling pretty good. The space that you make together feels cozy and safe. As time goes on, however, your consciousness becomes dependent on the other person, and that is when the situation becomes stressful. The boat that once felt cozy can start to feel cramped, and as one person moves around, the other may lose balance. That is how Elizabeth found herself in the water. Feelings and situations began to pile up on the couple until moving around without completely disrupting the balance of the boat became impossible. Elizabeth had become so dependent on her boyfriend to keep the boat balanced and moving forward that she had forgotten about her own ability to stay in balance. As life's information started to pile up in his boat, he could not continue to keep it balanced for both of them. He could barely find his own happiness and sanity in that cramped space. How could he keep her happiness and sanity for her, while he was struggling with his own? The pressure of managing the boat for two became too much for him. Elizabeth could feel that her balance was precarious, and the more chaotic their life together became, the more she tried to hold their relationship together. That only made the chaos worse because two people simply can't navigate one boat. While she was living her story dependent on her boyfriend, he was struggling to navigate for himself. He just didn't have the capacity to navigate for her, too. He kept nudging her, trying to get her to make room, but it didn't work, and before she knew it, he kicked her out of his kayak. Elizabeth suddenly found herself chest deep in the water with her kayak nowhere in sight. Putting the responsibility of your happiness on someone else is a lot to ask of anyone, and even the strongest of people have a challenging time making that scenario work.

The second part of Elizabeth's story deals with floundering in the water, getting back into the kayak, and then falling back into the water. After Elizabeth recovered from the shock of getting knocked out of her boyfriend's kayak, she spent some time treading water, trying to keep her head above it all. She was eventually able to find her kayak and get back in it, but as she tried to navigate through the information, she kept losing her focus and balance. She had let her boyfriend navigate for so long that she was no longer accustomed to processing information as her own. She found herself struggling to keep the information that she was calling in focused inward and directed at her heart. When she had been with her boyfriend, she let him take the lead. There were times when they would fight, or a conflict would arise, and they were always able to talk their way through to a resolution. As she looked back over the relationship, she could see information that she had ignored. She realized that over the past two years many situations had nagged at her, but she had simply pushed off the persistent feelings and ignored the information coming her way. Effectively, she had taken an extended emotional vacation in someone else's boat. She had gotten so accustomed to ignoring the information that had come up, that she created a pattern of putting everything her heart was trying to tell her on the back burner. She was not at all focused or centered in her consciousness. This pattern of not being able to be grounded and focused on her information is what caused her to fall out of her boat time and time again.

Elizabeth had to find her kayak and create a connection to her own story once more. If she was able to focus her attention inward, she could use what her heart had been calling in to help her. After a while, Elizabeth was able to reacquaint herself with what it felt like to be nestled in her own kayak. Being settled and balanced started to feel more natural. Eventually, she found that time between being in and out of her kayak got shorter. She was spending more time connected and less time in the water, till one day, she noticed she was floating downstream fully conscious and engaged in her life. It had become second nature to her, and she could not imagine ever giving her consciousness over to someone else again.

Now look at the details of how Elizabeth's story unfolded, and how she used the things that came into her life to eventually connect back to her heart, her story, and her freedom.

She could feel the rift with her boyfriend starting on a Tuesday. The weekend before had started fine, but they seemed to be falling out of sync. She knew that was typical for couples, and they had made it through rough patches before. Still, each time they struggled, they managed to resolve their differences. They almost always saw each other on Wednesday night. She would sleep over at his house, or he would stay at her house. They always spent the weekends together, and Wednesdays were a perfect way to break up the long week apart. They talked every day, but by the time Tuesday night rolled around, he still had not called her back. She went to bed wondering if he was okay. At this point, Elizabeth was more worried than angry. She called him in the morning and the call went straight to his voicemail. She wondered if she had forgotten about a big meeting that he had for work. She spent most of the morning with her mind preoccupied, wondering what had happened to him. She called him again at lunch, but again, the phone went straight to voicemail. She was now deeply worried thinking possibly he had been in an accident and was in a hospital somewhere. The possibilities swirled in her mind. Then, she picked up the phone and dialed his office. He always had an outgoing message that said the date. If it said yesterday's date, then she would call his parents and search all the hospitals until she found him. She was so worked up that she could hardly dial his office number. She waited for the ringing to stop, and heard his voice saying that it was that day's date, and that he was in the office but away from his desk or on another line. She hung up the phone without leaving a message and sat quietly at her desk for a while. She was glad it hadn't been yesterday's outgoing message, but at least that would have explained why he had been out of touch.

At that point, Elizabeth had been tossed out of her boyfriend's boat, and she was in shock. For those few still moments at her desk, she felt like she was sinking to the bottom of the river. Then her mind started churning, and her heart started hurting as her survival instinct kicked in. Elizabeth kicked her way up to the surface, and she started treading water in the river of her life with no boat in sight. Elizabeth's mind bubbled over with questions: What is my boyfriend doing? Is he going to leave me? What have I done to deserve this? Why can't he just communicate with me? If he could just tell me what to do, I could do it. All these thoughts played over and over again in her mind. They were supposed to be going out to dinner and had planned on staying at his house and watching a movie. What was she supposed to do now, she wondered. Should she go home? Should she go to his house? Should she call him again? By the time the workday was over, she had almost given herself a panic attack with all the questions and wondering. She was exhausted from treading water all day. She got into her car and didn't know where to go. She began to cry. She was frustrated and felt completely lost and confused. How could he do this to me? Why won't he just talk to me? Just then, her cell phone rang and his name flashed across the screen. Her heart jumped.

She picked up the phone and said hello. She could hear his voice reply to her, but he seemed so distant somehow. He asked her what time she was planning on coming over to the house so that they could leave for dinner. She shook off the tears, as if she had finally caught sight of his boat. Had she made everything up in her head? Was everything just fine between them? With those questions, she swam back to his boat. Without too much of a flinch, she replied to him with a time, and told him that she loved him, and that she would see him shortly. Just like that, she was back in the boat with him. She wondered what had happened to make him so hard to get in touch with. She spent a few moments getting freshened up before she headed over to meet him. She didn't want him to be able to tell that she had been crying.

She walked up to the house with her overnight bag in her hand, like she had done hundreds of time before. As she opened the door and called out his name, the puppy that they had picked out together came up to greet her. She began to feel like she was settling back in. She put her bag down in the entryway and walked back into the kitchen to find him. He was sitting at the bar with two glasses of wine. She smiled at him, kissed him on the cheek and sat down beside him. She took a deep breath and soaked in the reassuring environment that she had walked into. "Long day?" he asked her, as he noticed her sigh.

"It *was* actually. What about you, busy day?" she replied, hoping to find out why he had not responded to her.

"Not especially. I took the afternoon off and went to the park," he said.

"Oh, that explains why I couldn't get ahold of you. I started to get a little worried," she said.

"Oh," he replied.

She looked at him, puzzled by his evasion. In her mind she was thinking,

"Oh—*oh* is all you've got?" But instead of getting frustrated, she asked him what he did at the park.

"I just had a lot to think about, and I wasn't getting anything done at work. So, I took a personal afternoon," he explained. "Are you about ready to leave for dinner?" he asked.

"Why don't we just stay here? If you don't feel like being out, or you still have a lot on your mind, we can just order a pizza and relax," she offered.

"Listen, it's fine, let's just go to dinner," he said with a sharp tone that she had not heard before.

"Are you okay?" she asked, as she began to feel a little uneasy because of his tone.

"There is just no good way to do this," he said, as he stood up.

"Do what?" she asked.

"I was going to tell you at dinner, but waiting seems pointless. I tried to bring it up this weekend, but couldn't bring myself to say it," he said, not looking at her.

She began to feel disoriented. She could not wrap her mind around what it was he was trying to say. She quickly thought back over the weekend. She knew they were off, but what could he have tried to tell her? She couldn't figure it out.

"I'm done," he said, as he looked up at her.

"Done with what?" she asked, puzzled.

"Done with this. I am done with us. I talked with my mom about it again today and she was right. I have to be honest with you and tell you that I am done."

"You talked with your mom about us, and you didn't bother to talk to me about us. How does that make sense to you?" she questioned, feeling even more confused.

"We don't want the same things, Elizabeth. We could keep living this life together, getting by on the hope that one day we will be completely on the same page with what we want. But, I don't want to live that way. I want something more for myself, and for you, too. I don't want to spend time surviving something that is not working."

He was talking about children. She was not sure she wanted them, and he wanted them yesterday. She knew that the conversation would come up again, but she hadn't thought that it would come up as an ending.

"I don't want to keep living a life with you, not certain that we are the best thing for each other. I know there is a part of you that feels the same way. You have to feel it. Let's not just get by in life, because that is what this has become," he said to her from across the kitchen.

Tears had started to pour out of her eyes. It wasn't that she was crying—she was in too much shock to be crying. But, it was almost as if there was a faucet attached to her eyes, and someone had turned it on. She looked up at him, swallowed really hard to compose herself, and stood up.

"If you're done, then you're done," she said almost coldly. She walked to the door and grabbed her bag. Before she opened the door, she turned around. He had followed her and was standing right behind her.

"Are you sure this is what you want? Are you sure you are done?" she said, and then bit down on her lip.

"Yes, but you don't have to go. We can talk about it more. I don't want you to leave like this," he said, trying to mend the pain he knew that he was causing.

"If you're done, you're done. Me staying is not going to change that," she said, shaking her head. She looked into his eyes one last time. She could feel the sadness taking over every muscle in her face, so she knew she had to get out of there before she lost it. She opened the door, walked through, turned around one more time, and said good-bye.

She made it to the car before she broke down into a sobbing mess. On the drive home, she ran through everything again and again, trying to make sense out of it. How could he do this to me? How could it be over? She made it home, climbed in bed, and cried for hours. The pain she was experiencing felt so much bigger than any pain she had ever felt before. Her heart was completely shattered. She was disoriented, pissed off, sad, speechless, angry, and strangely lethargic, all at the same time. All she wanted to do was to sleep, but she couldn't. So for hours, she stayed cocooned in her bed, replaying their whole relationship, particularly that evening, through her mind again and again.

When she woke up in the morning, she felt hungover from all the crying. For a moment, it all felt like a dream. Then the reality came crashing down on her heart. She picked up the phone and called in sick to work. She looked at herself in the bathroom mirror and started to cry again, so she went back to bed. This is where she would stay for two days. She was lost in the river of her life, and with no boat in sight, she was having a hard time functioning. She would cry until she fell asleep, and then she would wake up and her brain would start replaying everything over and over again. She could not escape the thoughts. It was as if her head kept going under the water, and she could barely catch her breath before that disoriented feeling overwhelmed her again. It seemed to be a never-ending cycle, until some part of her battered heart finally pulled her mind in a different direction. "Stop floundering in this sea of nothingness," she told herself. "You are drowning in your own life. Enough is enough! It's time to start to figure this out," she said, as if she were coaching herself. Within that simple statement, she found a sandbar in the river where she could rest for a moment. Something her boyfriend said to her that night had stuck out to her, and now that her mind and heart could rest for a moment, she could give that morsel of information some room to grow. He said something about how he didn't want to just *survive* their relationship. It was hard to look at, but if she was honest with herself, she could feel a hint of the mere survival that he was talking about.

Elizabeth decided to take a shower. She wanted to wash off everything that she had been wading through for the last couple of days. If she was going to think about everything in a new way, she needed to feel fresh. She sat on the floor of the shower and let the water wash over her. She kept coming back to the statement about surviving. She felt so hurt. The pain made it hard for her to be honest with herself, but she knew she had to do at least that if she was ever going to be able to leave her house again. She thought about it. Had she been merely surviving? It was then, for the first time, she realized that she had been in his boat, surviving her life rather than living it. Had she been in the relationship in hopes that together they could thrive in life instead of just survive it? In a weird twist, had she instead found herself surviving her life rather than thriving? With these questions, she became more curious about how she had gotten to this place. All of a sudden, she had room to breathe again. At this point she reminded herself, "Just be tender with yourself as you figure this out and make sense of this information."

For Elizabeth, being in the relationship had created contrast between surviving her life and enjoying it. Her heart had called in the relationship so that she could see something beyond where she had come from. She had lived into her heart's capacity, and now her heart was ready to shift beyond that old capacity. For some reason, she needed to experience the feeling of being heartbroken. She thought about how that heartbreak was another area of contrast. To be this broken allowed her to see the contrast of surviving versus the wholeness and peace that she longed for. She had enjoyed and lived into what she now understood as the limited capacity of her heart. Because of the contrast, she now could see that, rather than just completely enjoying the relationship, there was a large part of her that had just been surviving her own life by being with him. Her heart was calling in the difference between surviving and thriving.

When Elizabeth was finally honest with herself, she could see that when she first entered into the relationship she had been merely surviving her life. As she and her boyfriend began to build their love for each other, she felt the shift from surviving to thriving, and she began enjoying her life. She wanted to live into that for as long as she could, so she gave up everything to keep it.

As Elizabeth explored her past, she could remember feeling that same sort of shift take place during college. She had survived so much of childhood that when she attended college she discovered a place where she was able to thrive. Although, there were times when she recalled giving parts of herself away so that she could "thrive." Back then, she felt the same weird sort of feeling that resembled surviving. Her heart's capacity had been even more limited at that point, but her heart was leading her to stretch that capacity. In college, school and the successes she celebrated, there became her identity just as her relationship had become her identity now. After school, she had thrown herself into an internship and job with the same intensity. She thought that each new milestone, which became the focal point of her identity, allowed her to thrive in the environment instead of just surviving it. Unfortunately, the reality was that, in handing over her identity, she was still just surviving. Her capacity kept shifting, and the contrast that her heart was calling in kept getting greater, but she was still just surviving. She had been asking her boyfriend to be with her to help her create an identity so that she could thrive, but she ended up giving away so much of herself that, once again, she was in a place where she was only surviving her life. Elizabeth's heart had been calling in this mirror of surviving and thriving in life for a long time, but now the contrast had gotten so great that she could no longer ignore the incoming information. Her heart's capacity had shifted during each of the experiences, but this was the first time she was able to consciously look at the information. She knew that if she was able to navigate through and embrace whatever her heart was trying to let go of, then she could find some inner harmony and be able to truly thrive within her story.

Elizabeth realized that by acknowledging the contrast and identifying what was being mirrored, she was halfway there. She knew that the trouble in the water had to do with being in someone else's boat. She also knew what her statement was about. She had asked her boyfriend to be with her, so that he could help her create an identity within her life where she could thrive, rather than just survive, her life. She was starting to see the contrast, and by acknowledging the difference between how she had been living and how she wanted to be living, it allowed to her to get closer to being able to shift her statement. She knew she was out of her boat, so her new statement needed be a picture of her in her boat. After a great deal of thought, she decided on a statement that she hoped would help get herself back in her boat. "My identity blooms from a place within my heart, and I thrive in my life as I live from this connected place within," she claimed for herself. It was a lofty statement, but she knew she had to think big if she was ever going to get back into her kayak.

Elizabeth was right about being close to her goal. She already had most of the information right there at her fingertips. She turned off the shower and dried off. She decided she still was not ready to put on regular clothes. She still needed to feel cozy and safe, so she put on a pair of clean pajamas. She walked into the living room and opened the curtains. She squinted through the bright sunlight till her eyes adjusted. It looked like a beautiful day outside. Even though she felt like she could only be a spectator to the beauty on the other side of the big picture window, she was grateful that she had come that far. She knew that at some point she would be able to open the door and embrace the beauty outside. But for now, she curled up on the couch and let her mind and heart sift through her information as she watched the sunshine and breeze playing on the leaves of the trees. She knew that if the pain she had been feeling could have some sort of purpose, then she could live through it. "Maybe this experience could be the end of just surviving," she thought. "How wonderful that would be.

Rather than surviving this breakup, it could have purpose and allow me to get to a place where there was a possibility to flourish." It was that thought that helped her turn her attention inward again, so that she could find the essence behind the statement that had gotten her lost in the water.

Elizabeth went back to the statement that had gotten her into trouble again: "Be part of my identity, so that I can thrive, because on my own I can only survive." She knew that variations of that phrase completely resonated with all the different phases in her life. She knew she had seen it in her current life, in college, and even in high school. She went back even farther and remembered it being part of her story as far back as elementary school. Still, she was having a hard time finding the exact first time that the statement had become part of her process, so she decided to look at the underlying essence of the statement in hopes that it would spark a memory. She wanted someone else to help her create an identity, because there was a part of her that believed that, if she was alone, the only thing she could do was just survive. She realized that the essence behind the statement was a belief that she was not enough on her own. Somewhere, her old information was telling her that she was not enough and could not be happy on her own. Somewhere, a wound had convinced her that this limiting statement was true. If you are not enough on your own, then if you happen to be on you own, you will be lucky to scrimp by and survive.

She wondered where she had learned that. She kept coming back to her mother and father's relationship. They had been very dependent on each other, but hated each other through that dependency. To this day, she still didn't know why they hated each other, and why they were still married if they hated each other so much. There was love there, too. It was twisted and gnarled by the pain they caused each other, but it was there. The paradox of their relationship had always been a little bit confusing to her. Most of the yelling had subsided with age, but they were still passive-aggressive toward each other. The tiny taunts that they gave each other were like paper cuts to the soul. She knew that the underlying information of not being enough on her own had to have come from their twisted ways of loving each other. In many ways, she could see how her statement fit their lives. Now, she just needed to find the first time that it had gotten transferred from them to her. At some point, she had claimed it as her information, and now, she needed to determine when that had happened.

Elizabeth closed her eyes and took a deep breath. Patiently, she went back into those feelings of not being enough and struggling. Like frames in a movie, she replayed parts of her history until she came across a memory that struck a chord. She must have been about nine or ten at the time. On Christmas Eve, she had fallen asleep on the couch. Her parents had started to argue about whether to leave her there while they brought in the presents, or take her to her bedroom. Her mother wanted to leave her there, sleeping in the glow of the Christmas tree, but her father thought it was more practical to take her to bed before they started. Her mother won, and she remained curled up on the couch while they brought all the gifts out and laid them under the tree. She was awakened by their arguing, but wanted to stay up in hopes of seeing Santa. Curled up on the couch, she opened her eyes enough to sneak a peek at what was going on. As they brought the gifts in, she began to realize that *they* were Santa. She remembered feeling a little crushed, but her parents were in their pajamas and the lights from the tree softened them in a way that made her very happy. They worked together to put out all of the gifts. Her mother handed her father the tools that he needed to put together a beautiful pink bicycle. She caught little glimpses as she peeked out from under the blanket. Her heart filled with such love and wonder that it diluted her disappointment that Santa had not come down the chimney to bring her the pink bike.

Elizabeth looked down at herself and realized that, even today, when she wanted to feel safe, she nestled herself under a blanket on the couch. It was weird and yet comforting that she found herself in the exact same position as she recovered her distant memory. Knowing that she was in a safe and comfortable place, she allowed the memory of that night to finish playing out. After her father finished assembling the bicycle, her mother brought out the plate of cookies that Elizabeth had prepared only hours before. Her father took a reindeer cookie off the plate and ate it. Her mother took the tree cookie and bit the top off, then placed it back on the plate so Elizabeth would see the evidence that Santa had come to visit.

To Elizabeth, this part of the memory seemed blissful. Her parents were constantly at each other, but to see them working together, drunk on the magic of Christmas, was so beautiful. They felt like a happy family. In that moment, no one was walking on eggshells, no one was arguing. It might have been because it happened after such a wonderful moment that the argument that was about to take place would hurt Elizabeth so deeply. Perhaps Elizabeth had let her guard down in those moments, or maybe she had fallen in love with the possibility of harmony. For whatever reason, Elizabeth started to feel sad as she tiptoed into the next part of the memory.

Elizabeth could feel her father picking her up. Her father's arms were so strong, and in that moment she felt so safe and loved. Her mother kissed her forehead and the three of them walked back to her bedroom. Her mother talked about how she hoped Elizabeth would like the pink bike, and how she wasn't sure if she should have gotten the purple one. Her father said that the pink bike would be just fine, and that Elizabeth would never know the difference, so it wouldn't matter. They placed her on the bed and tucked the blankets around her. Her mother talked about how wonderful Christmas morning would be, and her father agreed.

Then, with one statement, her mother took all three of them out of the blissful reality that they had created and placed them back into the reality that Elizabeth had been working to survive throughout her whole life. "We should have done more and made it bigger." Her father kissed Elizabeth's head and walked to the door. Her mother turned out the lamp and followed him. Suddenly, her father turned around and told Elizabeth's mother that she was crazy.

"Listen here, tomorrow morning is going to be wonderful. There is plenty under that tree to make any person happy, and I don't understand why it's not enough to make you happy." She remembered her father saying, "Nothing is ever enough for you. Do you realize that without me you would have nothing? Is that what you want to go back to? Because it can be arranged." Her father seemed to yell at her mother, even in a whisper.

"Oh, that's right, you're the be-all-and-end-all of this whole damn world. I am so sorry, I forgot for a moment," she spat back at him. "Go ahead and threaten to leave me out in the cold on Christmas, you ungrateful bastard."

"I'm the ungrateful one. Look around you. Look at everything thing that I have worked so hard to give you. It's because of me that you are not out working your tail off surviving somewhere. It's because of me that you get to have this fancy life that you always dreamed of but never thought you could have. And you think that I am the ungrateful one," her father argued back.

"You told me your dreams, and I made them happen," her father continued. "Where the hell do you think you would be without me? Certainly not sitting in a big house, tucking your beautiful child into her fancy bed on Christmas Eve. I have given you everything you have ever asked for and more! Without me you would have none of it! Just remember that!" her father whisper-yelled as he walked out of the room. Her mother followed behind him and shut the door.

Elizabeth could still hear their voices but could no longer make out the words. She felt a little stunned as she recalled that night. She had not thought about it in years. She definitely had not realized that it had affected her so deeply. That was the night when the wound was created. She knew that her family had never been perfect, but on that night, so much contrast had been created that the wound was undeniable. She listened to her father tell her mother that she would be nothing without him. As a ten-year-old, Elizabeth could not decipher what the truth or reality of the situation really was. All she knew was that it felt awful to be alone in that room. That little girl was just surviving the whiplash of having her joy and connection totally shattered. She didn't know how to make sense of this volatile situation, and she was afraid of what might happen next. So, from that moment forward, the new information that came into her heart would come in and have to filter through that wounded place. It was in this memory that she started to claim that she was not enough on her own. With everything that her parents had been saying to each other, how could she be enough? She would give parts of herself away in order to keep the peace or find some semblance of joy. Her identity and heart began to live in the shadows of other people and things.

Elizabeth cried as she realized that, all this time, her heart had been hiding in broad daylight behind school, and work, and her boyfriend. She knew what she had to do next. She had to go back and help that sweet girl. She could see her, as clear as day. She needed to connect with her and help her understand. She had to show her how to get back to the place where her heart felt full and connected, just like it had in the earlier part of the memory. She didn't want her to suffer any longer.

Elizabeth closed her eyes and went back to the glow of the Christmas tree. She sat by the fireplace as her parents finished getting everything situated. She could see the little girl's eyes peeking out from behind the covers, watching with such joy. She watched her parents carry her to her bedroom, and she snuck in and sat on the far side of the bed as the argument played out. Once the door was shut, Elizabeth could hear the little girl crying. That is when she made her move.

She crawled up to the head of the bed and touched the little girl's shoulder. "Elizabeth?" she whispered into her ear. "Can you hear me?"

The little girl nodded her head.

"Can you turn around and look at me?"

The little girl rolled over under the covers, and Elizabeth could see the tears that soaked her sweet little face. She could not help herself as she wrapped her arms around the little girl and held on to her until she stopped crying.

"I want to explain something to you. Do you think you can listen to me? It's very important," she said gently. Then Elizabeth sat up on the bed and helped the little girl get comfortable. She reached over and turned on the lamp, so that they could see each other better.

"I want you to know that the argument that your parents just had was not about you." She held the little girl's hand. "I need you to do something for me. Can you tell me what it felt like when you were on the couch a few moments ago?" The little girl shrugged. "Try to tell me everything that you remember about it."

"Well, it was like a fairy tale, or what I would picture in a story," she said with another sniffle. "Everything was so cozy. Mom and Dad were happy and helping each other. I could smell the pine tree and the fire in the fireplace. The glow from the lights on the Christmas tree sparkled, it was so beautiful," she said, with her heart so full it might burst at the seams.

Elizabeth giggled as she started her reply. "How wonderful. You know, you are an incredibly lucky girl to have gotten to witness that Christmas miracle."

The little girl cocked her head to one side. "I am?" she replied, questioningly.

"You sure are. You know, not everyone gets to see a Christmas miracle. That moment in time is something beautiful that you will have for the rest of your life. The glow of that Christmas tree and the sound of your parents laughing as they helped each other will stay right in there," she said, putting her hand on the little girl's chest.

"But what about all of the arguing? And what about everything that my daddy said about not having anything? I don't want that to be me. If it happened to my mommy, it can happen to me too, right?" she asked, as she looked up at Elizabeth. Before Elizabeth could answer, the little girl was declaring her decision. "I just need to make them happy again. If they are happy, then no one has to wind up with nothing."

Elizabeth looked down at the child and pulled her in closer. "The arguing is hard, and all of the stuff that your daddy said was hurtful to your mommy and to you, but none of that was about you! Their pain does not have to be your pain. We can't change the way your mommy and daddy are with each other, but I can tell you some secret truths about them that might help you understand. The secret truth for your mommy is that she has whatever she needs with or without your daddy. See, your daddy just really wants your mommy to see him and love him, but your mommy is always a little scared to give in to love because she is afraid it might just disappear. And, your daddy's secret truth is that he really has all of the love he could ever need, he just doesn't know it. Just like your mommy doesn't know that she has everything that she needs," Elizabeth explained.

"Wow! That is sort of like another Christmas miracle," the little girl said with a smile.

"That's right, it is. What if I make you a deal?" Elizabeth said, as she straightened the blanket around the little girl's lap.

"What kind of deal?" the little girl asked.

"A deal where I promise to be there to help you understand things when they get confusing. I will be with you to explain when your parents don't understand their own secret truths. And in return, you have to promise not to lose sight of the joy and connection that you found tonight," Elizabeth explained.

"Oh, I think that's a great deal," The little girl replied as she filled back up with joy.

"I have one more thing to tell you. It's about your secret truth. Do you want to hear it?" Elizabeth asked.

"Yes please," the child said, sitting up a little taller.

"This is your secret truth. I am connected right to your heart, and you are connected right to mine," Elizabeth said, putting the little girl's hands to her heart. "Whenever you feel separated or unsure of something, all you have to do is tap in to your heart and I will be there to help you," Elizabeth said.

"Just like our deal," the little girl said, excitedly.

"Yes sweetheart, just like our deal. Now that we have all of that squared away, what would you say to going to sleep so you can wake up to a beautiful Christmas morning?" Elizabeth asked.

"Would you stay with me and maybe sleep with me tonight?" the little girl asked.

"Remember, I am always with you. Tonight we will sleep together all cozy under the covers, dreaming about Christmas. How does that sound?" Elizabeth asked.

"Perfect," the little girl replied.

They tucked themselves in under the covers and, with their arms wrapped around each other, they fell asleep perfectly happy, connected, and filed with joy.

Elizabeth rested in this place of complete connection for a long time before she returned to the reality of her day. As she opened her eyes and looked around the room, she couldn't help but notice the smile radiating on her own face. In her entire life, she'd never felt this connected. She could feel the joy and happiness in every cell of her being. She not only knew that she could keep the deal that they had made, she looked forward to it. She had found the wound and had begun to shift it. She used the information that was coming up in her life as her own, and had found her heart, and her story.

Elizabeth was on the right track. She had tapped in to her heart and had successfully navigated through her information. She was back in her own kayak and basking in the joy and connection as she floated down the river of life. She was able to keep this place of consciousness, where she was grounded and balanced in her boat, all weekend. A few times, the feeling of surviving started to feel close to her heart again, but she simply turned to the little girl inside of her and loved her through those moments.

That part of Elizabeth's story demonstrates one example of getting back into your kayak after being knocked into the water. In the next part, you'll learn how being out of your kayak for a long time can lead you back into the water again. If your consciousness has been wrapped up in someone else for any length of time, you have created a pattern of looking outward at your information. It takes time and practice to change those patterns. Eventually, looking inward toward your information will become second nature, and you may even find that it feels like an adventure. Until you get to that place, it is not uncommon to find yourself splashing in the water again as you start to engage with the environment around you once more. The trick is to look at it as an exercise. If you find yourself out of your kayak, then take another look at all of the information and find your way back into your consciousness, and back into your kayak. Remember, no matter where you find yourself, you have the information that you need to get back up and into your boat.

Let's take a look at the next phase of Elizabeth's story. After days of grieving, Elizabeth was able to use her information to find her way back to her kayak. From there, she was able to spend a few days marveling at the freedom that her heart had created. The sadness was dissipating, and in its place she found a deeper sense of connection than she had ever experienced. She went back to work and found that when people asked about the breakup she was able to convey the freedom that she had been feeling—and that was that. Life hadn't skipped too much of a beat. A few days turned into a few weeks. Life was back in full swing, work was busy, and there were few moments that weren't filled with some sort of distracting tasks.

Elizabeth became preoccupied with all of the tasks in the flow of life. Because she was not completely used to looking at the things that happened to her or around her as "her information" or a reflection of her heart, she was missing them as they happened. Memories of her relationship filtered in, and her focus started to shift outward. Small things were happening that reminded her to connect with the girl who suffered the original wound. Her heart knew that she had been paying attention, so the volume had been turned down. However, as her focus kept shifting outward, she started losing herself in the memories and all of the tasks she had taken on. The original statement that she had been working toward embodying was slowly being pushed into the distance. "My identity blooms from a place within my heart, and I thrive in my life as I live from this connected place within." Her focus had shifted away from the statement and the ten-year-old, and had returned to the memories and tasks that she wanted to use to create an identity for herself. As the focus shifted, the volume started to dial up again until she found herself back in the water.

The information coming in had been pretty gentle until the drive home at the end of the week. Elizabeth needed to go to the grocery store on the way home, and she decided to take the back way home so she could have a more direct route to the store. Traffic was going to be challenging, but she didn't have anywhere to be, so she turned on the radio and rolled down the windows to help make the trip more enjoyable. She pulled into the parking lot, jumped out of the car, and headed inside. She was walking down the dog food aisle, thinking about the dog that she would no longer have in her life, when an old man rammed his cart into the back of her legs. Startled and a little in pain, Elizabeth turned around to face the man. Before she could even get a word out, he moved his cart past her and walked on to the next aisle. She shook her head in complete bewilderment. How could he not see her, or at least say something? A little agitated, she shook it off and finished her shopping. Even so, she couldn't stop thinking that she should have told him to watch where he was going. The backs of her heels still hurt as she walked to the car. This was the volume on her information getting turned up just a touch.

Elizabeth walked out to the car only to find that someone had stolen the radio out of it. She had left her windows down, thinking she wouldn't be in the store for very long. She could feel her blood pressure start to rise, and, by the time she got off the phone with the police and the insurance company, she was pissed. Even though there was no damage to the car aside from the absent radio, Elizabeth was highly annoyed about the hassle of replacing the thing. She got home and put her groceries away. As she put the melted ice cream away, she considered the end of her day. An old man had bruised the back of her heels, and someone had stolen her radio. "Seriously?!" she thought. She wanted to scream out: "How could you not see me? How could you take that from me?" Completely annoyed, she called it a night and went to bed. She was so distracted by the statements running through her head that she didn't realize how disconnected she had become. She was so agitated that she had a hard time falling asleep.

By this point, she was no longer in her boat. The information that would help her get back into her boat was right in front of her. But she was in the water, and her attention was on the struggle and not the information that had gotten her there. All she needed to do was turn her attention inward.

She had been focusing her attention on the old man and the thief who stole her radio, and what they both did to her. If she shifted her attention just a little, she could look at them and the situation that was created as a reflection of information that her heart was carrying.

She woke up in the morning feeling crushed. She wondered how all of this crappy stuff could be happening to her. She sat out on her back balcony drinking her tea and thinking about the contrast between where she had been just a few weeks ago versus today. She had been feeling more connected, and now, suddenly, she felt like she was back in the water, just surviving again. "Am I back to surviving versus thriving?" she asked herself. That one question was all she needed to help her change the focus and get her eye back on her kayak. After that, it was only a matter of time before she would be sitting in her boat once again.

She thought about the information for a moment. If it was less about the people in the situation and more about her, then she wondered what the link was between the old man and the thief. It took her back to feeling like she was surviving, but the information didn't seem to stop there. For the first time in days, her mind returned to the little girl with the wound, but in this case she felt safe, and she was not worried about surviving. Elizabeth realized that her connection to the girl had faded. It was hard to sit with her and sift through the memories of her relationship at the same time. She recognized that the distance she was feeling was part of the information coming in. Feeling connected to the girl had helped her feel connected to her own heart, but the guy in the store had run right over her, and the thief, in some respects, had done the same thing. He had taken something from her without a thought for how it would affect her. In a way, this kind of disregard reminded her that, in the course of the last week or so, she had not been connecting to the girl in her heart. The disregard resonated with her, but something more seemed to be trying to come to the surface. Every time she thought about it, she wanted to scream. The phrases, "How could you not see me," and "How could you do this to me?" kept coming up. Although she held back, she wanted to scream those words out. Eventually, Elizabeth realized that the essence behind both situations had to do with her being seen and acknowledged. To gain that acknowledgment, Elizabeth needed to have a voice. She decided that spending some time getting back to her kayak would be more than worthwhile. After all, the feeling of being in the water was less appealing now that she really knew what it was like to be nestled in her boat.

She knew that if the reflection of the information was that she was not being seen or heard, then she needed to shift her statement to one that established her voice. She came up with a purposeful statement and jotted it down on a piece of paper: "When I am in my kayak, I have a strong voice that reflects the connected place within my heart." She reflected back on all of the times when her voice had been usurped. She tried to remember the first time she felt the desire to scream out. Elizabeth found herself right back in her bedroom on Christmas Eve. As her parents were arguing, she wanted to sit up and scream at them to stop fighting. Before she got lost in what her parents were saying, she wanted them to stop and realize how beautiful the evening had been. She wanted to tell them to stop ruining it for her. But her voice was locked in fear. It was almost the exact same message that she wanted to shout out to them. "Don't you see me? How can you do this to me?"

Elizabeth was not able to stay in her kayak because there was another layer of information that was tied to the wound she had discovered after the breakup. Her current state in the water went back to the wound that had been created on that Christmas Eve. Losing her identity and surviving her life was the first part of the wound, and the second part was losing her voice. She had worked on shifting the part about her identity and the feeling of thriving versus surviving, but without going another layer deeper and claiming her voice, it would be impossible for her to stay in her boat.

If she was going to make true her new statement, "When I am in my kayak, I have a strong voice that reflects the connected place within my heart," then she needed to go back to that girl. She needed to help her find her voice, and reassure her that she would always be there for her. She would be there to hear her and see her. So, that is exactly what she did. Elizabeth closed her eyes and found herself back on the bed with the younger version of herself.

"So, my sweet little friend. You want to scream at them?" she said, turning the statement into a question.

The little girl looked up at her shocked. "How do you know that?" she asked.

"Because I want to yell at them, too," Elizabeth replied.

The little girl giggled, and put her head on Elizabeth's lap. Elizabeth stroked her hair for a moment as she thought of what to say next.

"You know what we should do?" Elizabeth asked, taking her little hands and pulling the girl up to face her. Looking into those big green eyes, Elizabeth's heart swelled with love. "We should scream." Before the little girl knew it, Elizabeth had pulled her up onto her feet and they were both standing hand-in-hand on the bed. Elizabeth started jumping up and down. "What is it you want to say?" she asked the little girl, as she coaxed her into jumping.

"Don't you see me?" the little girl said quietly, as she jumped.

"What else can you say?" Elizabeth probed.

"Don't you see how wonderful things can be? Stop fighting and see how beautiful everything is!" the little girl said, a little louder.

Elizabeth noticed that she had stopped asking questions and had started making statements. She knew this was a good sign. The two of them were laughing and jumping and shouting about how wonderful and beautiful everything was. They eventually tired and plopped down on their bottoms. Smiling at the little girl, Elizabeth asked her if she felt better. The little girl replied yes, and then reached over, put her little arms around Elizabeth's neck, and gave her a huge hug.

"I want you to know that even if they don't hear you, I do," Elizabeth said holding the girl. "No matter what, I see you and I hear you! Do you feel like you can be heard now?" Elizabeth asked her.

"I sure do," the child said, proudly.

"Do you feel scared anymore?" Elizabeth asked.

"Nope. I'm having too much fun to be scared."

"That's awesome," Elizabeth said.

Elizabeth had been able to go back and shift the second layer of the wound. With her new statement established as truth, she found herself back in her kayak and feeling completely connected. Her new truthful statement made her voice strong, as long as she was connected and conscious. As long as she held on to that place, everything she did would be a reflection of that shifted place within her heart. Now that she had found her voice, and was grounded in her own identity, she had room to thrive. She had done the work with the information that her heart had called in, and she had created even more capacity for her heart.

As she moved through the weekend, Elizabeth recognized that her life seemed more in sync. Everything felt a little bit easier. Even being on the phone with the insurance company was easier. The first time she called, she had spoken to an unhelpful person, which was no coincidence. This time the person made getting her radio replaced sound easy. As Elizabeth acknowledged the positive mirrors she was witnessing, she knew she was living into the new capacity of her heart.

Elizabeth went in to work on Monday, ready for the work week. She knew that she had several meetings with clients, and she felt grounded and prepared. Her whole morning was spent trying to calm down anxious people who didn't understand the numbers that they were being shown. She went straight out of that meeting in to a team meeting where her boss was freaking out about people not following though. By the time she took a late lunch, all she wanted to do was curl up under her desk. She decided to take a walk outside and get some fresh air.

She wondered how she had ended up feeling like she was out of her boat again. "This is ridiculous and frustrating," she thought. "I really hoped that the inner peace would be sustainable." Then she got a little curious about the information. Had she just taken on the frustration of the other people, or were they mirroring up something in her? she wondered. Was it that the girl within her was frustrated and worried that she would get lost in the work week? Was her heart calling in the frustration to create enough contrast so that she would not go back into the water?

All of those things made sense in Elizabeth's story and were probably part of the reason that her heart called in the scenarios. However, the more valuable information was that her heart was giving her the opportunity to change an old pattern.

Sometimes your heart calls in exercises to help you shift past old patterns that have formed as part of an old wound. If your mind has been processing and circulating information through the old wound in your heart for a long time, ruts have been created in your behavior pattern that were caused by the old information. Hence, out of habit, you may still end up reacting from the place where the wound once was. It is important to determine if the information is something new to navigate through or if it is an exercise to help you shift out of the pattern. When Elizabeth recognized the rut she had developed, she could see it as a gift, giving her the opportunity to change the old pattern of jumping out of her boat that was associated with the wound.

On her way back to the office, Elizabeth whispered, "Be tender with yourself," over and over again. After she returned to her desk, she pulled a picture out of her bag. Elizabeth had gone through a box of old photos and found one of herself as a child sitting under the Christmas tree. It was not from the same year as the wound, but it helped her tap in to her heart every time she looked at it. She had carried it with her, just in case she needed a reminder. She looked at the little redheaded, green-eyed girl sitting by the Christmas tree. "We can do this," she thought. She pictured herself jumping on the bed and giggling. "I am ready for the rest of my day," she thought. "I see you and I hear you my sweet, sweet girl!" Elizabeth said out loud. She smiled and realized that, in comparison to the first time she had to get herself back in her boat, this round had taken her a lot less time. She had drastically reduced how long it took from the point of being knocked in the water to getting settled back in her own boat. She also noticed that the information was much more gentle. She was consciously grateful for both of those improvements.

Elizabeth met with clients again that afternoon with much less frustration now, thanks to her awareness that the annoyance she felt was less about them and more about her. She had reconnected, and was balanced and flowing in her boat. She knew that she had the answers that her clients needed, and if she didn't, she knew that she could get them. She thought about her statement: "When I am in my kayak, I have a strong voice that reflects the connected place within my heart." Because she knew it was true, she could engage with the clients and trust that she would be able to help them from a connected place. By using her information, she was able to get back in her boat and reset old patterns that had been working against her, and she no longer needed to merely survive her life. As a bonus, Elizabeth was also able to build the growing voice within her heart.

In Elizabeth's story, you can see what it was like to navigate through being knocked out of someone else's kayak and climbing back into your own. Elizabeth's story also illustrates that it may take some time to figure out how to stay in your kayak. If you find yourself in a similar scenario, try to be tender with yourself and curious about the information around you. You have all that you need to find your way back to consciousness.

CHAPTER 6

Patterns, Scenarios, and Voices

ᘓᗧᗧᗧᖰ

A S YOU CONTINUE TO AWAKEN TO YOUR STORY, the opportunity to find and move through information will become second nature. Using the mirrors and reflections in your life as well as incorporating the Stream-Kayak Principle will help you identify and navigate through just about any situation and the old information associated with it. As you navigate and move through your story, you will need to be alert to three other methods of identifying your information. Patterns, scenarios, and voices may also become instrumental in identifying and navigating through your information. These three tools may tear at your mind and heart, making you view them as negative and detrimental to your happiness. However, with an inward perspective, you can give them purpose and use them to help you. A pattern starts when a thought repeatedly follows a particular path within your story. As you continue to follow that same path over and over again, a pattern is created. Scenarios are similar, and may call upon the patterns that you are engaged in, but their main purpose is to act as illustrations for what your heart is feeling or calling in. Voices may also call upon patterns, but their purpose is to narrate what is in your heart. Like most of the perspectives in *Awakening to Your Story*, the key to growth lies in turning your attention inward and becoming curious. Only through curiosity can you find understanding. As you look more deeply at these three tools, you will learn to identify each one and how it can present itself in your story.

Patterns

LET'S START WITH IDENTIFYING PATTERNS. A pattern is created when a thought runs a complete circuit over and over again in your mind. A good analogy to this starts in a park with a lush field of green grass. If people walk repeatedly over the grass in the one area, the grass will wear away until you can see a pattern form. Following that path becomes natural to people who visit the park. Your mind is like that field of grass. If a thought is formed and carried through to the same end result enough times, or with enough emphasis, a pattern is created. Once the pattern is created, the most natural thing to do is to follow that pattern as it is laid out for you.

When patterns start from a place of being wounded or an old pile of information, they create a path associated with that old wound or pile of information, which keeps you linked to living in, and reacting from, that place. When you survived the situation or place where the wounded information was initiated, a pattern began to form, teaching you that the way you survived is the best way to engage with situations similar to that original one. The development of that survival mechanism is actually quite brilliant. The problem is that, as you shift your information, your heart's capacity also begins to shift to a place beyond the limitations of survival. The old pattern might have been effective at the time the wound was created, and might still be effective if you are living through the old wound. However, if you are shifting the old wounds out and broadening your capacity for happiness, then you will find that the old patterns no longer serve you well.

You may recognize a pattern as you are trying to shift your information, or the recognition may be an indicator of information that is ready to be shifted out of your story.

You may find that you are struggling to change the pattern. You may have navigated through the information in your mind, and feel as though you can embody the shift in information. However, if you are struggling to change the pattern, your heart may still be responding to the old wound. Remember, it is all just information, and your life is an adventure, not a race. With this in mind, you can make the pattern productive. Rather than struggling to change the pattern, use the struggle to help you change. If the old pattern continues presenting itself in the same way, your heart may be calling it in as an exercise to help you fully embody the change your heart is making. You may notice the change as a subtle shift in perspective, but even that may have a profound impact on your story.

Think of it like this: You have worked to shift your information. Your mind and heart are on board. You feel less reaction to the pile of wounded information, and you feel pretty good about the new pattern you are creating for yourself. Picture the green field with the old path of travel worn down to dirt. Now, walk another path. Just because you walked the new path once does not mean that you have created a pattern distinguishable enough to recognize it when it is put in contrast to the old path. It takes time and usage for the new pattern to become familiar enough for you to recognize it. The more you walk down the new path, the less you are using the old, allowing the grass to grow back—the old pattern fades away. The patterns within our stories are the same. Shifting information and walking through that shift is incredible, but it is only your first step into embodying your new capacity, like walking through the grassy field on a new path for the first time. To fully embody the change, your heart will call in exercises so that you can walk down your new path and create your new, healthier pattern—one that reflects the harmony you are shifting toward. You will have the opportunity to choose what you now know as your heart's truth and make a conscious choice to step out of the old pattern and into the new one. You may notice the exercises right away, and they may even feel to you like the volume is being dialed up. But, they are not there to hurt you—they are there to help you. It is not a test that you can fail, but an exercise designed to help build the new pattern. Engage in these situations with curiosity, determination, hope, tenderness, and love for what you are creating.

As your patterns shift into healthier ones that are serving you well, they will embody that downstream flow. Your mind will run along the currents of connection, compassion, and love. The healthy patterns help you find answers and information that direct you even deeper into harmony with yourself and the world around you. They serve as indicators of your strength and depth of connection to your heart and your story.

Scenarios

SCENARIOS ARE LIKE WAKING DREAMS. They are the images that play out as your mind drifts. You might be driving in the car or working at your desk when they play out. They can be created at almost any moment and reflect the inner workings of your heart. They act as short plays that illustrate and bring life to what resonates within your story. Scenarios can be active or passive in nature. When they are passive, they pop up and pop out without you even noticing them much, almost like a release valve for your heart. When they are active, they can have more volume associated with them and may more overtly demand your attention.

While scenarios can be active and passive, they can also illustrate dreams or patterns. In addition, depending on your perspective, they can be detrimental or helpful to engaging in your conscious life. When illustrating dreams, they can be like fairy tales that your heart yearns to experience. When illustrating patterns, scenarios can bring images and stories to mind that shine a light on the patterns you hold.

Scenarios that illustrate dreams are helpful because they give you the opportunity to become more conscious of what it is you are longing for. It's like opening a window to your heart's desire. If your heart is dreaming, then you are creating movement to a new level of capacity. The dreams signify that your heart is ready to start calling in information to lead you to the place where your dreams can be realized. This can be a valuable tool to bring consciousness to the direction your heart is leading you toward.

Scenarios also illustrate what it is you want to create within your story. This is where you have to be careful not to live into the scenario, but rather live into the movement toward that waking dream or the essence behind the dream. It can be easy to get lost in the details of the scenario that plays out in your mind. When an image matches your heart's desire it can be hard not to become attached to an outcome associated with that image. Scenarios are windows to your heart's desire, not doors for you to walk through. When you try to use scenarios as doorways, you inevitably find yourself lost, resenting the people around you for not living into your dream with you. You may also find that you become more frustrated and wind up paddling upstream trying to force your reality to match your waking dream. Remember, it's a window, not a door. It is there to help you identify what it is your heart is longing for or needing.

Once you recognize a scenario is playing out in your mind, take the time to separate the details of the dream from the undercurrent or essence. It can be easy to get lost, or find yourself living outside of what is real, but if you pay conscious attention to finding the purpose for the scenario, then you are that much closer to bringing it into your reality. Remember, the scenario is there to be an illustration for what your heart wants to create, not to distract you from creating movement toward it.

Scenarios that illustrate patterns create images that help us understand the patterns that our hearts are carrying. If your patterns are healthy, then you may find yourself daydreaming about moving easily and harmoniously though life. You may see pictures of yourself basking downstream as life works in your favor. You may also play scenarios over and over in your mind that keep you tethered to old wounded patterns and information. These can be distracting and destructive. By giving this kind of scenario a purpose and viewing them as indicators, you turn them into tools that can help you understand what it is your heart is longing for.

If you find yourself lost in images that are tied to old patterns, you should determine whether they are providing new information that needs to be navigated through, or offering you exercises meant to help you shift your old information and create a new pattern. If the scenario points to new information, go back and navigate your way through it just as you would if you were navigating according to the Stream–Kayak Principle. If the scenario appears to present an exercise of a newly-developing pattern, look the challenge in the eye. Consciously choose to let go of the old pattern and step completely into the new one that you are creating. Remember, as long as you use a scenario, it can help you move closer to a deeper sense of connection and harmony.

Voices

VOICES ARE NARRATIONS OF WHAT LIVES WITHIN the space of your heart. They may play out as echoes of voices from people who have affected your life, or they can manifest as your own voice. You may notice them as whispers talking to you as you go along with your everyday life, or they may be shocking, loud, nagging voices that try to attract your attention. When given purpose, they can be great indicators of where you are within your story. When left without purpose, they can be utterly distracting.

When the voices narrate harmonious dialogue within your heart, they feel encouraging and help keep you motivated to stay connected within your story. However, when they give voice to old negative information, they can feel crippling. They may tell you things that you are fighting not to believe, but the more you hear them, the harder the statements are to disregard. When the voices are loud, you need to get curious. Focusing inward and giving purpose to the negative voices is not only informative, but also empowering. Find out what the voices are expressing. Are they trying to help you re-pattern, or are they pointing to information that needs your attention and navigation? As you curiously dig in, remember, the information being provided is less about the person behind the voice and more about what the information is trying to tell you. What is it saying? How are you reacting to it? Do you believe it? What emotion does it bring up for you? When is the first time you experienced that emotion? Find the undercurrent, and use it to navigate your way through. That one tiny negative voice, when given purpose and used correctly, can unravel limiting negativity that has you locked in a place of stagnant challenge.

As you can see, your perspective is the key to growing and moving past the old wounds. If you use what comes into your space, you have an unlimited supply of opportunity to create movement within your story. Every event in your story can potentially help you, rather than harm you. The outcome depends on how you utilize the information and circumstances. Remember, this is your story and you have the opportunity to live into it completely. Patterns, scenarios, and voices show you how to step up and take an active role in living completely into your story. Using them as tools can create a shift that will manifest in your mind, heart, and body. This is where you can make big leaps forward, living into your new capacity. Awakening to your story is only the first step. The greater leap is living into your story every day of your life.

Glossary

awakening to your story – 1) The act of waking up and consciously engaging with the information within your life and story. 2) The process of shifting your perspective inward so that you can recognize the circumstances and situations in your everyday life as neutral information that is there to help you get where it is you want to go.

call in [information] – Your heart has the capability to "call in" all of the information that you need.

cellular memories – A cellular memory is a memory that when recalled, triggers a response in the core of your being.

consciousness – The level and ability to be awake and aware of all the aspects within your story.

contrast – The difference between where you are versus where you would like to go. This gives you the opportunity to see what it is you want versus what it is you have. Without contrast, it's hard to know what it is you want.

curiosity – The capability of looking for clues that can direct you to your information.

downstream – When you are in sync and flowing along the current of life, the feeling of bliss and happiness through which your heart feels full—sustainable when conscious and connected to your heart. (Element of the Stream–Kayak Principle.)

expectation – The belief that a specific event will or should happen in a certain way.

filter through [old information] – Your perception of new information is distorted when it *filters through* old information.

harmonizing your heart – Embracing your current information and navigating your way through the old, which allows you to be completely connected and conscious. This creates a space for you to be in harmony with your story and smoothly flowing downstream through life by removing wounds found in the old piles of your information.

heart capacity – The space in which your heart can hold harmony and all things positive. As you dream and evolve emotionally, this expands and gives you the opportunity to live into the new, increased capacity.

heart-space – Same as *heart capacity*.

hiccup – Small negative information that keeps coming up contributing to troubles in the stream of your life.

Indicators – Clues within your story that point you in the direction of pertinent information.

information – Anything that comes into your story. Everything that comes into your life can be useful information.

interacting – When you respond to information that comes into your story from a neutral place and a place of harmony within your heart.

kayak / boat – The metaphorical vessel that each person gets to travel in, afloat along in the river of life. You have everything that you need within your kayak, and your vessel represents your consciousness (Element of the Stream–Kayak Principle).

lift up [information] – To move information aside so that you can see past it and overcome it.

mirrors – People or circumstances in your life that are used as figurative or circumstantial mirrors. When you look at the information behind them, it helps you see the reflection of the inner working of your own heart.

navigating – What you do with your information if you find yourself reacting to something within your story or if you find yourself having any sort of trouble in the river of life. Step three of the Stream–Kayak Principle describes the process of navigating—moving—through your information. Phase A – Identifying Your Statement; Phase B – Creating & Acknowledging Contrast; Phase C – Consciously Shifting Your Statement; Phase D – Gathering Information; Phase E – Harmonizing Your Heart.

neutral information – Information that comes into your story, and your everyday life, and does not bump up against the old piles of information.

old piles of information – Information that has accumulated from your childhood, adolescence, and young adulthood. When the information comes in, but you are not equipped to sort through it at the time, it begins to pile up. When this happens, the new information has to either filter through the old info, or you end up reacting to the old information as it comes in.

out of your boat – When you are out of your kayak floundering in troubled waters, and struggling to survive the current of the river of life—unsustainable. (Element of the Stream–Kayak Principle.)

patterns – Thoughts that run repeatedly along a pathway within your story. When a thought is carried through to an end result enough times, or with enough emphasis, a *pattern* is created.

projection – A version of reality that you cast onto someone else.

reaction – A response to information that comes into your story and everyday life through the wounds held within your old piles of information.

reflections – The information that is reflected back at you from figurative or circumstantial mirrors.

river of life – A metaphorical river that represents your life. Naturally, just as in nature, it flows downstream. When you are in harmony with the universe and all that you are surrounded by, you flow downstream with it. (Element of the Stream–Kayak Principle.)

scenarios – Images that play out as your mind drifts, they act as illustrations for what your heart is feeling. They are like waking dreams.

shift [information, statement, story, etc.] – Movement or change.

statements – Your vocabulary applied to your information. A statement can reflect the information in any form; one that needs to be shifted or one that reflects the evolution you are trying to create.

Stream–Kayak Principle – A set of rules and supporting processes designed to help you identify where you are in relationship to your conciseness and information, and to manipulate your position and direction in order to attain a harmonious state of being.

tools – Anything that you can use to help you create evolution, growth, and movement within your story, or that can help you get to where it is you want to go.

two people in one boat – When two people try to fit into just one of their kayaks, it may be comfortable or comforting at first, but it is unsustainable for the long haul. (Element of the Stream–Kayak Principle.)

undercurrent – The essence of the information that you are utilizing. When you boil the information down, and take out all the circumstantial noise, you are left with the part of the information that you can use as a tool.

upstream – Struggling or fighting against the natural flow of the current of life—unsustainable. (Element of the Stream–Kayak Principle.)

voices – They narrate what is within your heart. Can be your own voice or may be echoes of someone else's information that you claimed as your own along the way.

wound – Damaging information that you are holding on to that is limiting your heart's capacity to live positively into your fullest expression of life. Wounds are created by situations from the past and can be subconscious in nature.

www.ingramcontent.com/pod-product-compliance
Lightning Source LLC
Chambersburg PA
CBHW022024090426
42739CB00006BA/274